Praise for *The Architecture of Image...*

"Park has captured for all of us in the AEC industry the essence of what it takes to be successful developers and marketers of our brand—a heretofore little understood concept in the industry. His book should be required reading for every client-facing member of our firms from new grad to CEO."

—JOE BROOKS
Director of Corporate Marketing
Burns & McDonnell

"I wish I had access to this book when I was leading my firm through a new branding initiative. No one has a broader, more researched perspective of marketing professional services. When Park speaks... listen; when he writes... read."

—BILL VIEHMAN
Former Chief Marketing Officer (retired)
Perkins+Will

"A must read for anyone responsible for developing, protecting, and promoting a firm's image and brand. Park points out why firms need to do more than be different from the competition. It's more than theory, it's about getting results and Park provides the pathway."

—MITCHEL LEVITT, ACHE, FSMPS, ASSOC. AIA
Senior Vice President & Director of Market Strategies
FKP Architects

"After dispensing with the basics of branding—and what it is not—Park offers far-reaching and wide-ranging illustrations of how to enhance your firm's image. The book serves as a useful checklist for the many ways that you can impact your brand."

—HOWARD J. WOLFF
Most Senior Person
Full-Height Advice, Inc.

"As a nationally recognized master of marketing A/E services, Park takes a fresh and fascinating look at the whole concept of branding. His book guides you to a highly effective approach to evaluate and implement a brand strategy. A must read!"

—PATRICK BELL
President
Patrick C. Bell & Company

"Anyone who really wants to differentiate themselves in this competitive market environment needs to follow Park's approach—to the letter. He articulates the importance of a brand better than anyone I know."

—JOHN L. WHISLER, JR., PE
Vice President of Engineering and Construction
KS International

"Park has done a great job of organizing all the basics about what a company's brand is and how it specifically relates to the A/E/C industry. His book should be an essential read for anyone hoping to start their own practice or be an owner in a large firm."

—J. PETER DEVEREAUX, FAIA
President and CMO
Harley Ellis Devereaux

"Branding is how you present and reinforce your identity through consistent messaging of the image you have created. Park's book provides excellent ideas and anecdotal support of these concepts."

—RANDOLPH W. TUCKER, PE
Associate Principal, Fire Protection/Life Safety
CCRD

"It takes a bold and wily veteran marketer to tackle the issue of brand in today's complex market. Many ponder the 'new normal' and wail about commoditization. Park does not waste your time dwelling on the companioned misery so many enjoy. His book speaks to action and will lead you to masterful branding success."

—SCOTT BRALEY, FAIA
President
Braley Consulting & Training

"Considering the importance of getting your company's brand recognized in today's fast-paced, modern culture, Park's book is designed for success. I thoroughly recommend it as an addition to your branding toolbox. Applying Park's guidance will help your firm make the transition from ordinary to extraordinary."

—ED KASPAREK
Senior Vice President & Director of Global Business Development
Thornton Tomasetti

"Dispelling the myths of what branding isn't, Park provides a laser focus on what many have found to be an elusive and mysterious concept for professional service firms and gets to the heart of the matter of effective branding. Drawn on real-world experiences from his exemplary career and those of other marketing legends, the examples provided, advice cited, and recommendations made can make an immediate and lasting difference."

—JUDY L. HRICAK, CPSM
Vice President & Chief Marketing Officer
Gannett Fleming

ALSO BY CRAIG PARK

The Architecture of Value: Building Your Professional Practice

AS A CONTRIBUTING AUTHOR

Marketing Handbook for the Design & Construction Professional

A/E/C Business Development... The Decade Ahead

The Architecture of Image

Branding Your Professional Practice

Craig Park

Foreword by
Ron Worth, CAE, FSMPS
CEO of SMPS & Author of *Building Profits*

AquilanPress
Reach New Heights

ISBN# 978-0-9893382-0-2

For more information, contact:

Craig Park
402.609.6131
craig@craigpark.com
www.craigpark.com
www.thevirtualcmo.com

Published by:

Aquilan Press
www.aquilanpress.com

Cover Photo:

Getty Center Blue, **2002 by Craig Park**

For My Elusive Muse

TABLE OF CONTENTS

FOREWORD i

INTRODUCTION | *This Brand's For You!* v

PART I - CULTURE | Your Brand *Begins* 1

CHAPTER 1 | **Discovery** 13
   BRIGHT OPERATIONS: *The Trusted Advisor* 31
CHAPTER 2 | **Assessment** 33
   MulvannyG2 Architecture: *Value and Passion* 45
CHAPTER 3 | **Authenticity** 51
   BNIM: *Walking Their Talk* 63

PART II - COLLABORATION | Your Brand *Builds* 67

CHAPTER 4 | **Acumen** 75
   GEOTECHNOLOGIES: *The Personal Network* 89
CHAPTER 5 | **Maturity** 93
   GILBANE BUILDING COMPANY: *Family Matters* 101
CHAPTER 6 | **Evolution** 105
   HGA: *A Culture of Collaboration* 113

PART III - COMMUNICATION | Your Brand *Becomes* 117

CHAPTER 7 | **Expression** 125

RATIO Architects: *A Promise of Integrity* 141

CHAPTER 8 | **Resonance**...145

WET: *Remarkable* 167

CHAPTER 9 | **Results** 171

PSI: *One Company, One Call*...193

AFTERWORD | You Are *The New Black!* 197

RECOMMENDED READING 203

INDEX TO CONTRIBUTORS...207

BRAND WEB LINKS..209

ACKNOWLEDGEMENTS 211

ABOUT THE AUTHOR..215

An idea that is developed and put into action is more important than an idea that only exists as an idea.

BUDDHA

FOREWORD

If you are not a brand, you are a commodity.
PHILIP KOTLER

IF YOU DO NOT HAVE A KNOWN AND RECOGNIZABLE BRAND, I predict
your firm won't be around in another decade. Professional
services—and those in the design and construction industry, in
particular—are changing at a rapid pace driven by the 'new
normal' economy of this post-recessionary period. If you haven't
found a way to segment your firm and create a distinctive brand
in today's new resource-challenged, hyper-connected world, I
worry for your future.

Commoditization has hit the service industry hard and is
pushing many firms to either merge or liquidate. Better, those
leading firms finding new specializations and creating unique
brands continue to grow and prosper.

Which will you be?

The Architecture of Image

Today, your firm must be prepared to meet the challenge of reduced work, increased competition, and limited resources head on with focus, creativeness, and sheer determination in order to win, let alone survive.

In *The Architecture of Image*, Craig Park shares insights into some of the profound and innovative ways companies are meeting this challenge. The best practices that are illustrated here are truly exemplary. He shows what some of the best and most successful firms are doing.

However, just reading about them won't change your future. Nor will copying another firm's model is no guarantee for the future you seek. This book provides the guidelines you need to create your own memorable brand. Seriously study the methods outlined here and adapt them for your own use. Then you can forge ahead with confidence in your own vision and your own brand.

While certainly challenging, we live in truly exciting and dynamic times with unimagined changes occurring almost daily. As a result, service firms must be nimble, innovative, and willing to try new processes outside of your comfort zone. No company can take the demand for its services for granted. New technologies are dramatically influencing all aspects of the way we pursue, develop, and build relationships and create buildings today. As a result, your brand message must resonate across many mediums.

Every client has a strategic choice as to which professional firm best meets their needs at that given time. As each client is unique, each project is even more complex and demanding to meet the occupants' wants and desires. At the same time, your service must provide you a return on its investment of time and resources. This is where your brand becomes critical. By differentiating on value, your brand provides the foundation for mutually beneficial business-to-business relationships.

Organizational structures are different now for both our clients and our own firms. Most are much flatter than before the Great Recession. New lean and more efficient methods of procuring and developing work have altered past hierarchical management styles, pushing the decision making to a smaller set of participants. Your clients can obtain information about your firm that they never dreamed of being able to get before. This provides even more reason that your brand must be recognizable and easily researched, and appear at the top of any search list. Is yours?

The Architecture of Image

Craig has always been a visionary and futurist within the design and construction industry. His writing and speaking inspires many.

His first book, *The Architecture of Value: Building Your Professional Service,* was an intellectual look at the 'big picture' of professional services, and is recommended reading for those seeking SMPS' professional certification.

In *The Architecture of Image*, Craig again provides an excellent road map for you to follow. Take the time to study this book. Make sure your fellow leaders read it as well.

Those wise enough to listen to his message on branding and follow the guidance he provides will prevail. It will definitely help your brand to be successful in the years ahead.

— **Ron Worth,** CAE, FSMPS, CPSM
Chief Executive Officer
Society for Marketing Professional Services
Alexandria, VA

INTRODUCTION | *This Brand's For You!*

Create a sense of urgency, excitement, vibrancy, a buzz.
TOM PETERS

BRAND HAS BEEN THE BUZZ WORD in the professional services marketing world for the last decade. But many firms still struggle with the concept. What is your company's brand?

You read and hear a lot about branding, but virtually all of the published literature and Internet citings are associated with products, services, or retail environments in the business-to-consumer sector. There is very little published specifically about the brand created by the services of a professional advisor or licensed consultant working in the business-to-business space.

For the professional service firm, your brand is *feeling*. Your brand is *impression*. Your brand is *perception*. Your brand is a *reflection*—of your culture, how you collaborate, and how you communicate.

I wrote this book to help you explore how to define, develop, and enhance the brand of your professional service firm.

For a professional service firm to plan, grow, and endure, it is critical to understand how your brand is perceived internally and externally. Having an understanding of the many aspects of brand value is important before you can effectively start a brand-building program.

THE ELEMENTS

Your brand is composed of three related, but separate elements. The first is *brand identity*, or how you and your employees see your company and its service offerings. Identity is informed by your vision of what you want to become in the future.

The second element is *brand image*, or how your clients, customers, vendors, collaborators, and potential clients view your company. When both identity and image are in alignment, you have a strong brand.

When they are disparate, your brand is weak. When they are aligned, your brand has authenticity and the foundation for building the third element, *brand equity*.

Equity is the most important aspect of your brand. It is the intrinsic financial benefit your brand brings to the fiscal value of your practice, positively or negatively.

Here are three big ideas I want you to take from this book:

1. **For your brand to be successful, it has to *begin* as authentic. Your brand reflects your *culture*.**

2. **Your brand must *build* on your history and reflect your practice. Your brand demonstrates how you *collaborate* as thought leaders with your clients and those allied in your field.**

3. **Your brand should also challenge you to move beyond what you know and allow you to *become* what you want to be. Your brand is how you *communicate* your vision, framed by your reality.**

Your brand is defined by what you do, how you do what you do, and how you act as you do it. The importance of those actions extends to everyone in your organization—your culture. Their actions have the power to define, build, and communicate your brand by how they:

- **Impact your clients**
- **Influence your clients' clients**
- **Inform your communities**

The well-integrated brand recognizes that each of these actions is reflected in the perceptions and recognition of your brand.

The diagram at left illustrates the confluence of industry, regional, and popular brand recognition. The scale of each set within the diagram is indicative of the brand value as measured by your surveys of brand recognition. The complement—or union—of each set shows your brand value in your industry, regional market, and community. This same analysis can be extended to multiregional or even international sectors. The complements are defined as:

- **Industry Recognition**—Your firm is acknowledged for unique and specialized knowledge, and experience based on research and practical applications, as demonstrated by completed projects.

- **Regional Recognition**—Your firm is the 'go-to' company for the press and the professional communities for research, publications, and presentations in your areas of expertise.

- **Popular Recognition**—Your firm contributes to important community efforts through volunteerism, sponsorship, and charitable participation that visibly benefits the larger populous.

The services you provide, the ideas you bring to a client, and the value those solutions deliver—the *"what"* and the *"how"* of the *"why"* of your service—define your brand. While there is no simple formula to building the brand of a professional service practice, this diagram of the integrated brand illustrates those values common to the strongest brands. Developing, sustaining, and expanding your brand is a complex process.

THE CHALLENGE

Working in professional services, one common theme you hear at virtually every marketing event is the critical need to differentiate. Your peers and competitors—the other consultants, regardless of specialty—usually complain that they are constantly being commoditized by their clients.

Organizational strategist, Marjanne Pearson, president of TalentStar explains, *"The challenge for the professional service firm is that telling your story is like trying to communicate the amorphous to the uninformed."*

The Architecture of Image

It often seems very difficult for your clients—the public and private sector organizations who hire you—to differentiate one firm within a given service sector from another. This is the fundamental challenge of the professional service firm's brand and why understanding service branding is so important. The ultimate goal of your brand is to have every client in your sector talking about your firm in positive terms.

Your brand is not what you think you are. Your brand is what everyone else thinks you are, and, most importantly, what they think *about* you.

The result of a successful branding program is consistent and continued positive feedback for you and your staff for what you do and the value you bring to your clients.

WHAT YOUR BRAND IS *NOT!*

Too often graphics are confused as the sole definition of the brand. Be clear:

- Your brand is *not* a logo.
- Your brand is *not* a color.
- Your brand is *not* a tagline.
- Your brand is *not* your brochure.
- Your brand is *not* your website.

Although each of these graphical elements are important as part of a brand program—and the how and why for them is addressed later in the book—they are decidedly not what define your brand. While graphics are critical for business-to-consumer product placement, they are definitely only a small part of professional service identity and image.

This is not a book about graphic design, collateral development, or website motif. There are many other authors much better at helping you with those challenges.

Before you ever get to the graphic look of your brand, you need to understand what your brand really is. This is a book about building a strong brand that is based on who you really are.

THE PREMISE

The Architecture of Image is the second book in the *Architecture of Practice*™ series. The first book—*The Architecture of Value*— focused on strategy, story, and delivery, and became recommended reading for the Society for Marketing Professional Services CPSM accreditation program. Subsequent books in the series will explore leadership—*The Architecture of Vision*—and, technology—*The Architecture of Connection*. My goal is to provide you with insight and best practices that will lead to the creation of a successful and lasting professional service venture.

The fundamentals of creating an enduring professional practice parallel the practice of architecture—where collaborative teams conceive, design, and document a solution to a client's challenge, and coordinate in the execution of that solution: the build—thus the title for the book and the series. My goal is that these books become a useful tool and reference for professional service firms.

While my experience comes from working in the design, engineering, and construction sector, I believe this same need for building a strong professional service brand through culture, collaboration, and communication is common to other service-oriented businesses. Differentiating your firm from another is based on knowing who you are, how you are perceived, and communicating your expertise—your thought leadership— every day.

The lawyer, doctor, advertising agency, accountant, or financial advisor all need to find a compelling story that conveys the passion they bring to their practice and their clients, and the creativity their expertise and experience affords.

As a result, their clients develop a brand image from working with them. So, think of the design, engineering, and construction-related references as metaphors for all professional services that provide intellectual property as their product and trusted advice as their brand promise.

A LITTLE HISTORY

In 1972, Congress passed the Brooks Act, which established and mandated a qualifications-based selection (QBS) process for securing the professional services of an architect, engineer, or contractor. This act still applies to all Federally-sponsored projects and by practice has extended to many public institutions' and private organizations' selection processes.

However, today—under the guise of being prequalified based on their expertise and experience—many firms still find themselves in a one-of-three—or -four, or -five or -six—shortlist of choices, requiring a 20- to 45-minute dog-and-pony show just to get to the negotiations table. Only then do they find themselves in an often painful, and too often profitless, price-based haggling.

The Architecture of Image

Worse, even with the mandate for QBS, engineers and consultants often find they are still selected based on price alone as the prime consultants strive to eke out even a marginal profit.

Architects may have a slight leg up on the engineers and contractors in this selection process because the product of their efforts is more visual. Architects and designers have a portfolio of images—built or un-built—of their buildings and spaces that can convey their brand identity.[1] A few firms like Gehry Partners, Richard Meier & Partners, and Barbara Barry Inc., exemplify brands known for their iconic sense of design.

Engineers, for the most part, have a harder time, because most of their work is invisible; buried within the walls and structure of the buildings on which they work. Too often, the contractors work is as much a reflection of the architect and engineer, in the minds of buyers of service, as it is about their skills as builders.

In the end, the brand is defined by the service each firm provides. The ideas they bring to a project and the quality of the service they provide to the client—the what and the how of the who they serve—defines their brand.

---

[1] A good example is Gehry Partners, whose notable projects, like the Walt Disney Concert Hall in Los Angeles, shown on the cover of this book, established their brand for iconic design.

SIZE DOES NOT MATTER

A brand is not only the sole property of the large firm. The same need to establish differentiators and to build trust for service applies to businesses of all sizes, from the sole practitioner to the multi-office, multi-national firm.

A successful brand can be very localized, if that is where you chose to focus your practice. Your brand can be as regional, national, international, or even intergalactic, as your vision allows.

Learning to convey and communicate the nature and value of your service is equally important. The key is to not just differentiate, but to be distinct—distinct in the level of expertise of your staff, distinct in the delivery of your service, and distinct in the experience the client has working with you.

It is difficult to find anyone not under the influence of contemporary advertising media typically associated with a brand. Internet, radio, television, billboards, magazines, and newspapers inundate our daily lives. Little of this style of brand development or promotion has relevance to the professional service firm.

As a result, I have focused this book on the best practices for firms engaged in providing intellectual, advisory, and creative services to their clients and who are committed to building a strong and enduring brand.

THE CONTRIBUTORS

The writing of *The Architecture of Image* benefited from the expert input from several industry leaders.

The significant contributions of my editor, **Tracy Black**, president of Black Cape Marketing, add a unique perspective of someone technically trained in architecture, but who has practiced most of her highly successful career as a leader in marketing professional services.

As the manuscript evolved, her insights on the importance to your brand of the connection between your firm, your clients, and your community, inform the entirety of the book's perspective.

You will find her experiential expertise on brand valuation in *Assessment;* pursuit strategies in *Authenticity;* the importance of graphic standards in *Expression;* and, the importance of credible metrics in *Results.*

Finally, her editorial guidance added important clarity to my writing on this often challenging topic.

Throughout the book you will find citations drawn from my interviews with several nationally recognized brands' marketing leaders, including:

- **Tom Boogher**, *executive vice president* with environmental and testing engineers, **PSI**

- **Ann Banning-Wright**, *president* of management consultancy, **Bright Operations**

- **Tim Barrick**, *principal* with architects, **RATIO Architects**

- **Julie Luers**, *vice president and director of marketing* with architects and engineers, **HGA**

- **Maria Maffry,** *vice president* of business development with architects, **BNIM**

- **Teresa Powell-Caldwell**, *vice president* with water-feature design and manufacturing specialists, **WET**

- **Mike Savage**, *vice president* with geotechnical and geology engineers, **Geotechnologies, Inc.**

- **Carla Thompson,** *global marketing director* for **Mulvanny/G2 Architecture**

- **Chris Watson**, *national director of marketing* for builders and construction managers, **Gilbane Building Company**

Each of these experts shared their perspective drawn from real-world branding experience. They represent views ranging from a sole practitioner to the senior members of large organizations that work locally, regionally, nationally, and even internationally.

Following each chapter you will find profiles of each of their firms that illustrate what they see as critical to the brand process. From small, locally successful firms, to large, highly integrated practices, to internationally known specialists, each of these firm's brand stories share a common theme.

There firms each started with an individual or small group of cohorts with a personal vision that leveraged the power of their passion to build a highly successful brand in their area of practice. Today they demonstrate how the theoretical has been applied to the practical to establish their brands' value.

This cross-section from the architectural, engineering, and construction fields consists of firms that are admired not only by me, but by the building industry and their clients. Their unique brands reflect both their focus and their values.

In addition, **Ron Worth**, chief executive officer of the Society for Marketing Professional Services and author of *Building Profits in the Construction Industry*—who also kindly penned the book's foreword—and public relations expert **Mike Reilly**, president of Reilly Communications, shared their thoughts as recognized leaders in the field of brand marketing.

The book also includes insights from two of the Top 100 national branding firms[2]—drawn from interviews with **Richard Wilke**, *senior partner, global business development* at Lippincott in New York, and **Dick Musil,** *senior vice president and principal marketing strategist* at brand designers, Webster in Omaha— where they imparted their global perspective on the concepts and issues facing firms wanting to build a strong brand.

These anecdotal stories of some of the building industry's most interesting brands show that most successful firms, regardless of size, geographic reach, or aspiration, understand the importance and value of a consistent branding program.

THE POWER OF THREE

The Architecture of Image is divided into three major themes — Culture, Collaboration, and Communication—and three major actions—Begin, Build, and Become. Nine chapters set out the best practices for beginning, building, and becoming your own unique brand.

---

[2] Based on Graphis Magazine's 2012 annual rankings of the "100 Best in Advertising"

These themes and actions define the overarching issues facing the branding of your firm. Each chapter focuses on important processes for creating and sustaining an enduring brand. The sections in each chapter describe the theory, strategies, and tactical efforts needed to establish, maintain, and grow your brand.

The organizing premise is based on the *"the power of three."* This is a concept that resonates within management, operations, and most importantly, marketing. It stems from your culture, connection, and communication with new clients and extends to your relationship with existing clients.

Contemporary American philosopher, Ken Wilber, of the Integral Institute, espouses the power of three as dimensions and perspectives of good (morals), true (science), and beautiful (art).[3] This simple set of three comparators relates directly to the brand promise of the professional service firm.

Wilber's concept is that all aspects of practice, personal or professional, can be viewed in the relative measure of good versus bad (subjective), true versus false (quantitative and objective) and beautiful versus ugly (qualitative).

[3] Wilber, Ken, *A Theory of Everything: An Integral Vision for Business, Politics, Science and Spirituality*, Boston: Shambhala Publications, 2001.

Applying Wilber's integral model to the professional service practice, speed is measured as good, cost is always true, and quality conveys the subjective measure of beauty, or value. Where these three elements align in balance, there is trust and a brand that is strong.

Where they do not coincide (i.e., where focus on only two aspects diminishes the effectiveness of the third), there is misalignment. The customer's experience will be less for that lack of balance and the brand will be weakened.

Presentation basics emphasize using the power of three when giving a speech: First, tell the audience what you're going to tell them. Second, tell them. Third, tell them what you told them.

A Venn diagram, as show earlier, can be used as a simple tripartite illustration of the relationships between three sets and three complements, which yield a common value or goal at the nexus of the circles.

In defining your brand identity, three creates a series—a pattern of cause, effect, and result—the challenge, the solution, and the outcome, or the benefit, relevance, and proof of the work you do.

In telling a project or client-related story, use the power of three to set up your premise, explain the benefits, and prove it. In describing a differentiator, mention three attributes.

Three resonates with the listener and the reader. The human brain finds it easy to understand threes—in graphic design, it is how we organize elements, colors, and fonts. Most visual communication can be reduced to these three features.

Using the Power of Three to define your brand message, your brand will be stronger, and psychologically more potent.

MY BACKGROUND

Trained as an architect and practicing as an advisory consultant for most of my career, I have worked as chief marketing and strategy officer for several large firms. Much of my thinking comes from the lessons learned in leading the strategic efforts that focused on positioning those firms to win significant opportunities, create great projects, and build lasting client relationships.

The practice of architecture focuses on collaborative problem solving. It is a practice, when done well, that is—in Wilber's "integral" theory—thoughtful (good), well-documented (true), and creative (beautiful). These same concepts can be applied to professional service branding. The power of an integral approach to brand development is a cornerstone of this book.

In today's high-expectation digital age, clients have redefined the old service delivery mantra of *"cheaper, better, faster"* to a more aggressive expectation of *"free, perfect, and now."*[4] This premise takes direct aim at the outmoded advice of "pick two" and challenges you and your practice to deliver on all three.

Knowing that any one book can't cover it all, a bibliography of referenced and other recommended reading is included for your continued quest to learn about building a strong brand.

THIS BRAND'S FOR *YOU!*

The goal of my book is to help you build your brand through a better understanding of: your culture's and your clients' perceptions, and to communicating your differentiators to your clients, potential clients, and communities. As a result, you will build a strong and enduring brand and continue to grow an enduring professional practice.

— **CRAIG PARK, FSMPS, Assoc. AIA**
May 2013

---

[4] Rodin, Robert, *Free, Perfect, and Now: Connecting to the Three Insatiable Customer Demands*, New York: Free Press, 2000.

The Architecture of Image

PART I
CULTURE | Your Brand *Begins*

The right culture helps you succeed in accomplishing all your goals.

PEG NEUHAUSER

To UNDERSTAND YOUR BRAND, you first must understand your *culture*. To do this takes a journey of self-discovery of your firm's *identity*. Follow this with an assessment of your firm's position and *image* in the market. Finally, end with an evaluation of the *alignment* between your firm's identity and its image.

Understanding your firm's culture helps determine the core of your brand's identity—how you see yourself today and tomorrow. The culture of your firm—how you care for your staff, how your staff treats each other, and how the firm takes care of its clients, your clients' clients, and your communities—exemplifies the basis of your brand.

Is your company considered fun to work with and fun to work for? Or is your firm considered bureaucratic, boring, or bloated? You probably have elements of both. The list of potential adjectives is long. This first step of brand building requires an honest self-assessment of who you are as a professional service firm.

Ron Worth, CEO of the Society for Marketing Professional Services, says, *"The idea of brand promise and brand value is not leveraged enough in the professional service industry. Brand is what you are. Mission and vision are what you want to be. When the attributes you promise are different than how you are perceived, that can be confusing."*

Like the programming effort that begins almost every building project, the first step in understanding your culture is based on *discovery*—an honest look at your practice's current brand. This includes the development and description of your vision (aspiration), mission (deliverables), and the values (the enduring *how* and *why*) of your practice.

Richard Wilke, senior partner with international global brand strategists, Lippincott, comments, *"The good news for professional service firms is that their universe of clients is not typically as broad and vast as consumer companies, and you can reach them with a focused communications plan. I think the best counsel is to take the emotion and the politics out of it and look at it from an external market perspective to determine where the brand's strength truly lies."*

Dick Musil, senior vice president and principal marketing strategist with brand designers, Webster, says it equally well, *"If the people within your company don't understand what the brand represents—their mission, vision, values—there is very little chance they will accurately communicate it to your clients. A brand is not necessarily what you think it is; it is what your client thinks it is and what they understand. That is what is most important. If they don't understand what your brand is, you have a much more difficult job to differentiate your firm from your competitors."*

The next step in leveraging your culture is *assessment*—a reflection on your image. Your identity is based on your practice of the practice; how you want to be known and what you do. Your image is based on the perception of your clients—how they experience working with you. Together they define the reality of your brand.

The Architecture of Image

In Wilke's view, *"The very use of the term brand is something that needs to be clarified. Part of me says to just throw it out completely when you're talking to professional services and use words like, 'How are we perceived?' or 'How do we want to be perceived?' and 'What things should we do to make sure that happens?' That kind of a conversation is a lot more effective than, 'Let's talk about our brand.'"*

Carla Thompson, global marketing director at MulvannyG2 Architecture, says, *"Having everyone understand your brand must be a conscious part of the practice. Your company is only as good as your people."*

The review of your culture's identity and image concludes with a determination of the *authenticity* of what you inherently promise your clients when they hire you to deliver your service. In developing a differentiator for a professional practice, authenticity is critical. Alignment between your identity and image creates an authentic brand.

Having a strong, coherent way of presenting your organization and your capabilities has become incredibly important in professional services.

For many years, the idea of brand was just for the business-to-consumer companies or the really big business-to-business companies like Microsoft and IBM. Over time, law firms, accounting firms, investment banks, and design and engineering companies of all sizes have recognized that they need to project a strong and well-crafted brand in order to compete.

When identity and image are disparate, you will have work to do to overcome the misconception. Alignment is defined by how you practice your practice. As your firm matures, there is a natural progression of your brand—strengthened by time and experience.

HGA's vice president and director of marketing, Julie Luers agrees, *"We use brand as a differentiator. With so many good firms for clients to choose from, our message focuses on our leading-edge research, our open-mindedness to change, and our approach to collaboration."*

Teresa Powell-Caldwell, vice president with water feature designers, WET, says, *"While we follow firms like Apple as examples of living the brand, we know we define our own brand. We are on the leading edge of innovation. Clients who come to us want something that has never been done before."*

In summary, you can't look at someone else's brand and say we want to be like that. Take the time to find your own. You have to be true and authentic.

INTEGRATION

Building a strong brand requires a commitment to three basic concepts.

1. **First,** you must acknowledge that branding is a complex and continuous process—from the start of your practice through multiple generations of ownership.

2. **Second,** the brand must be integrated into the performance of all parts of the firm. It is not just a marketing effort.

3. **Third,** the brand must clearly demonstrate value authentically —internally to and by each member of the firm and externally to your clients, your clients' clients, future prospects, consultants, media, and the communities in which you serve.

Luers notes, *"The challenge is to make every employee engaged in and aware of the importance of understanding the brand. In this competitive market with more fee pressure, the benefit of a strong brand goes right to the bottom line."*

Mike Reilly, president of media relations strategists, Reilly Communications, agrees, *"Cultural awareness is a struggle because many firms concentrate decision making and strategy in a small group a people at the top."*

With social media playing a more important role in internal and external communication, firms have to extend beyond that small group of people to have everyone understand the brand message and value of how they perform their work. It is recognized that brand is a business advantage. You have to define the return on investment of your brand for your employees to execute their work in a way that supports your brand strategy.

DIFFERENTIATION

Unique! Value-based! Collaborative! Innovative! Cheap at twice the price! These are all (well, maybe not *all*) good descriptors for the differentiated firm. Again, it's not what you say about yourself. It is what your clients and the marketplace say about you. My guess is that what you won't hear from your clients is *"award winning," "stable,"* or *"established."*

What you want to hear is that you have a clear identity aligned with your market image. You offer specializations that are rare and service levels that are exemplary. Your marketing messages are thoughtful and client facing. You offer distinctive competencies. You are invested in project delivery. You understand client needs and issues. You are a partner in building success for your clients' businesses, their clients, and your communities.

True differentiation comes from remarkable and memorable attributes that *they can't get anywhere else!* This not only enhances your brand, but creates barriers to entry for your competition.

Powell-Caldwell, says, *"Remarkable can be good or bad. At WET we are remarkably good. Our projects stop people dead in their tracks."*

As Maria Maffry, vice president of business development at BNIM, points out, *"Our primary goal is to create such strong relationships and brand recognition that we are placed on a client-generated 'invited list' that at least minimizes the competition of conventional RFQs."*

One of the benefits of having a strong brand is that you become more definable, differentiated, and distinguished. Brand is the value of your firm relative to other business-to-business companies. A strong brand ensures you are always on the request for proposal list. If you already have a strong brand, it is about creating the perception of being a bit better or more desirable, all other aspects being equal.

Worth notes, *"The concept of brand for the professional service firm is critical. The underlying theme that has emerged out of the economic downturn is differentiation. Most firms have learned that commoditization is real, and the key to counter low-bid thinking is to be distinct. Unfortunately, most clients view the firms in the building industry as one in the same. The only firms that have escaped that perception are those that are distinct within their niche or that offer an exceptional capability."*

EQUITY

Brand equity is the financial value that is added to a service firm for its brand name compared with the value if the same service did not have the brand name.

A strong brand allows your firm to receive premium prices from clients. Fundamentally, it is the impact your people (culture), your practice (collaboration), and your marketing (communication) have on clients' knowledge and expectations.

Mike Savage, vice president with Geotechnologies, Inc., agrees, *"Brand equity represents the character of your firm, how you conduct your business, and the level of quality you deliver."*

A firm with a strong brand demonstrates such high value in the minds of their clients from the performance benefit, quality of service, or cost savings—in the best case, all three—that they are willing to pay more because they know intuitively that their expectations will be exceeded.

Brand equity is one of the factors that can increase the financial value of a company to its ownership and, ultimately, to anyone interested in investing in or acquiring you firm. Equity contribution can be measured objectively by growth, year over year, or by any of your key financial performance indicators.

Subjective elements of brand equity in your analysis include:

- **Brand language associations used by clients and the press**
- **Clients' perceptions of service quality and other relevant brand values**
- **Market recognition of thought leadership and expertise**

It is generally accepted that clients hire people they like, trust, and with whom they enjoy. Your brand provides a preview for what it is going to be like to work with your firm for new clients.

It also shows what's good or bad, based on their past experiences working with other firms.

For existing clients, your brand serves to remind them about that experience, and about your value—what it is you have that others may not."

Wilke concurs, *"I think a really important point for professional services firms to understand is that it's all about the people. In today's professional services marketplace, clients have become much more educated as buyers. They know the difference between the name on the letterhead and the people who are going to work on their projects. A lot of the firms have matured, and the people in these organizations are, in fact, the brand."*

Worth adds, *"To ensure your brand permeates your culture, the message has to be consistent from the top down. When a strong CEO or group of principals leads by example, the whole firm understands the value of the brand."*

ON CULTURE

It is critically important to imbed the concept and the importance of brand message within your culture. The enduring principles of a brand define how your services fit in the competitive marketplace in which you practice.

Reviewing each in context with your practice allows you to determine how your service is defined in your market, evaluate your aspirations and those of your people, and find what it will take for your brand to become respected.

CHAPTER 1 | Discovery

Discovery consists of seeing what everybody has seen and thinking what nobody has thought.
ALBERT VON SZENT-GYORGYI

THE FIRST STEP OF BRAND DISCOVERY starts with an understanding of your firm's vision, mission, and values. These should be the foundation of the firm's strategic plan, business plan, and marketing plan.

Discovery is accomplished through the practices of observation, analysis, and objective evaluation. It answers three fundamental questions:

- **Who are you now?**
- **Who do you want to be?**
- **What will you do for your clients to reach that goal?**

Through an examination of needs, desires, economy, and projected growth, discovery is stated from your perspective and those that serve under your brand. It defines your vision and passion for your service and is at the core of your brand promise. It is through this discovery process that the professional practice can really understand how it is communicates its brand.

For a building, the discovery process or program sets the guidelines for the design of the project. For the service firm, the discovery phase defines the potential for the brand. The process of articulating your vision, assessing your mission, and setting guiding values for your practice is the foundation for creating a strong brand.

Regional, national, and global opportunities start with a local focus on building a client base. While your aspirations may be for world domination, your firm's initial image development comes from serving key clients close to home. Those relationships create opportunities for future geographic growth.

It starts with a vision—an idea for a service that responds to a need. It is one that you are uniquely qualified and capable to fill. Fundamental economic analysis is critical. Too often, the aspiring practitioner will set up shop only to find the demand for their service is waning or their competitors got there first.

An inspirational vision—one that looks toward a horizon beyond your current view—provides the direction for your enterprise, defines its value and values, and drives the enterprise's purpose with motivation.

Does your firm have a strategic plan with a focus on your vision looking three to five years ahead? A business plan focused on your mission and goals in the next one to three years? A marketing plan focused on your brand and strategies looking to the year ahead?

Each of these plans must have actionable tactics and measurable results, with someone responsible to see the effort through. How many of you have that now? Some of it? None of it? Or do you hear, *"Plan? What plan? We don't need no stinking plan!"*

Do you monitor progress on a monthly basis? Quarterly? Annually? Ever? Too often, even those firms who take the time to create a plan leave them on a shelf to collect dust.

Mike Reilly says, *"Promoting your brand's vision, mission, and values is hugely important. Clients can't tell service firms apart. Clients need help understanding what makes a particular firm distinctive. Unfortunately, they typically don't get much help. Step one is to declare what your vision/mission/values are and then imbed that into your brand, whatever that brand value is."*

These basic business processes ensure you know where you are going, how you hold yourself and those you work with accountable, and how you know when you get there.

You should enter strategic, business, and marketing planning efforts with a goal *to see in yourselves as something you hadn't thought of before.*

WHY A BRAND?

The concept of brand is not only relevant to retail products or businesses. While there is much written on brand importance in the business-to-consumer marketplace, the focus here is on the brand of a business-to-business enterprise.

Webster's Musil says, *"One of the differentiators between branding a B2C product or retail experience from a B2B professional service is that the former is based a little more on emotion, whereas the latter is based a little more on logic. When you are dealing with a professional service practice, you often deal with what I call 'the point of presumption' that everyone knows what they do and how much different their practice is from everyone else's."*

He adds, "Those firms need to realize that they are in a marketplace where they have to brand themselves accurately and market themselves in a way that differentiates them from their peers. They have to become less analytical and more dynamic by offering a marketing message that has more life and energy. Professionals are very analytical people and they often wrongfully assume that their clients are analytical too, and that is not always the case."

When you hear, *"But we are not a grocery store!"* in reaction to a brand campaign discussion with a service provider, you realize that they do not see the importance of conveying a clear and consistent promise and that their brand is totally dependent on delivering on that promise.

VISION

Practice. Patience. Persistence. These three essential qualities—each needed to deliver a professional service regardless of market focus—are keys to the success of your brand.

Mastering your craft sets the bar for the practice and establishes barriers of entry for competition. Establishing a long-term vision and strategically planning toward a desired future sets a timeline for success. Recognizing that change is inevitable, diligence and fortitude allow for continued growth.

Entering in the professional service industry requires requisite skills, whether learned in school or through experience. It is the continuation of the former and the wisdom gained from the latter that exemplifies the best in any endeavor.

Where *vision* sets overarching goals for the future, *mission* defines what your practice delivers today. *Goals* establish objectives. *Objectives* define strategies. *Strategies* establish tactical action. And, *tactics* are the what, by when, and by whom that bring strategies to fruition.

Strength of character—defined by vision, integrity, and communication—is the fundamental nature of the leader. Creating, sustaining, and growing your practice will be a reflection of your firm's leadership and their ability to convey their vision. When uncertainty and setbacks undermine plans, the ability to rearticulate vision and set a new course is the hallmark of the best in class.

Continual education and application of learning, measured and steadfast action, and perseverance in the face of change will enable your practice to succeed. Leverage all three and your practice and brand will become what you desire.

Your *vision* is an expression of your aspiration—*what* you want to become, based on your expertise—stated in the present tense. This creates a positive reinforcement of your will to achieve your goal. It should be the foundation on which your practice is created—the *why* of what you do. It sets the tenor to all for what you want to achieve.

An example for a design firms' vision might be: *"Through design, we transform our clients' real estate assets into market-driven properties able to capitalize on untapped demand."*

MISSION

Your mission is your service—what you do today and every day to serve the needs of your clients. It is framed as a *result* based on what they *want* from you. It should speak to and inspire your clients. It tells the world who you are, what you do, and where you do it. It is your elevator speech.

Carla Thompson shared MulvannyG2's mission statement:

> *"Through our belief in trusting client relationships,*
> *we deliver unparalleled value through inspiring design,*
> *market leadership, and consistently dependable results.*
> *We hold ourselves accountable for design excellence*
> *and business performance to ensure our long-term*
> *future."*

This is a clear and succinct definition that sets the tone for MulvannyG2's brand promise.

The practice of your practice defines your mission. It is the services you offer, the geography you serve, and the client-types you target. A mission should be concrete, simple, and easily understood. The best mission statement frames your service description in terms of benefit to the client.

The mission statement is a chance to differentiate your service from those of your competitors. Most clients cannot easily distinguish between two service providers of the same discipline.

For many clients, any architect looks like an architect, any engineer looks like an engineer, and any lawyer looks like a lawyer. The specialization, locale, or industry leadership can be used to define your delivery in unique terms. Better, the size and scale of results delivered set you apart from the pack.

The mission statement is something everyone in your firm should know. It is fundamental to the *"why we work here"* that each employee should be able to answer. They should be encouraged to tell your story whenever and wherever possible. Imagine if every employee enthusiastically described your practice and its benefits to two or three people each week — neighbors, parents of their children's friends, and people they know from community and other professional or personal associations.

The impact of this type of viral marketing—everyone telling everyone they know what you do and the benefits you bring to your clients—can have a substantive and positive impact on your brand. Telling your story should never be left only to your business developers and marketing staff. Telling the brand's identity is everyone's job.

Your mission is *not* just the *who, what, when, where,* or *why* of what you do. It is not, *"We are 100 years old, with 1,200 people, and 30 offices, doing anything for anyone."* You might as well say *"We may be expensive, but we're slow"* or *"We are old, but we are tired."* Who wants to be known as being *"big and old?"*

A better example comes from national independent technology consultants, The Sextant Group: *"The Sextant Group supports owners and architects with demonstrated expertise in strategic technology planning, infrastructure design, and systems design for the realization of intelligent buildings."* That is a directly and succinctly stated mission. What is yours?

VALUES

Your values are the foundation on which your practice is based. Value statements establish the expectation of performance— internally and externally—for your service. Value statements frame what is important in your culture.

BNIM's Maffry, says, *"Our firm espouses deeply authentic values. We share our values with every new employee and apply those same values in our own practice, in the way we live, and the way we collaborate."*

The values that guide your practice further define your brand identity. They demonstrate an innate understanding of the culture you have created—how you behave, what is important, and what measure of quality and service you ascribe to the work you do. You should have as few as three and as many as five or six; and, like your mission, they should be memorable. They define the expectations you have for the practice of your practice. They are the foundation for building a strong brand.

Your firm's values should align with your market's expectation for service. They should not just be catch phrases like, *"We are the best at what we do."* Compared to what?

STRATEGIC PLANNING

Strategic planning is a well-accepted process to define a future state, create a roadmap to achieve it, and discover and share values. Setting goals, defining objectives, determining strategies, and assigning tactical responsibilities provide a road-map for your vision for the future. But where does that vision start?

In most companies, the vision and mission are driven top-down. The leaders set the path and the staff executes the plan. Closed-door sessions yield results-oriented plans, but too often tactical methods are ill-defined, and ill-measured. The challenge that firms who take this approach have is getting a cultural buy-in for their vision. Values are best defined and exemplified by the culture. Polling all staff for *"what is important about what we do for our clients?"* can illuminate how your practice sees value.

A bottom-up, inclusive, and integrated model delivers greater buy-in and exceptional benefits. Consider an initial whole-firm survey. Then engage a cross-section of the client-facing staff (marketing, business development, project management) combined with the process-facing staff (design, documentation, production), and vetted by quality-facing staff (assurance, compliance)., This type of *big-picture* discussion provides a methodology where the entire organization is engaged and committed to strategic success.

YOUR CULTURE

The process of identifying cultural values should be used as the precursor to strategic planning, as it sets the tone for the firm's current brand identity. It can also flag those issues that must be addressed to meet leadership's long-term goals.

When leaders see a fully-committed organization working toward a common set of goals and driven by innovative strategies, they inevitably see extraordinary results. This can be disconcerting for those who practice the traditional, hierarchal, command-and-control management style.

Musil, adds, *"The firms that have dynamic leadership who 'live the brand' are the most successful. Management has to live the brand. Bottom line is that with a good brand, a rising tide raises all boats: all aspects of the company benefit from a strong brand, not just the marketing and sales team. The stronger your brand is, the stronger your company is, and the stronger your position is in the market and the industry. It starts with great leadership."*

Values are core beliefs that remain true over time. They frame everything you do and how you do it, no matter where you decide to go. You should know what your core values are. They can include inspirational phrases like:

- **Quality**—We provide excellent quality service to our clients and deliver positive fiscal results to our stakeholders.
- **Effectiveness**—We maximize the effectiveness of our client's building programs benefiting occupants through sustainable design.
- **Integrity** – We safeguard the integrity of project delivery to meet our clients' fiscal goals.
- **Empowerment** – We empower our staff to achieve our firm's vision and mission, and to exceed our client's goals and objectives.

Many firms claim to have the similar values. Would anyone say that "integrity" is not one of theirs? It is important to communicate how your culture uniquely expresses those values that define the delivery of your service (e.g., the quality delivery of projects to meet client fiscal goals, as noted above).

Others might include *collaboration, passion,* or *innovation,* but each firm's core values are their own.[5]

Maffry notes, *"Over time, our core values have remained the same as when the firm was founded, but our mission and vision have evolved as the practice of the architecture evolved."*

First, identify what is truly different about your firm, process, clients, and employees. What is significant and notable? What do clients say? If you don't know, you have to ask.

Discovery is all about knowing what your practice wants to be, what it is now, and how—through expertise, diligence and delivery—it will establish the identity of your brand. The first step in any building project is creating a strong foundation. For your brand, discovery leads to the expression of your foundational values.

---

[5] For additional information on planning and an comprehensive look at values, see Greg Bell's excellent book, *Water the Bamboo: Unleashing the Potential of Teams and Individuals,* Three Star Publishing, 2009.

KNOW YOURSELF

To pursue work for the sake of work will often weaken the brand. In a challenging economy, when evaluating opportunities, the answer always seems to be *"Go!"* Should it be? That's the real question.

Competition for professional services, even in good times, is defined by the functions of expertise, excellence, experience, and the ability to deliver *relevant* solutions. This is even more important today, with limited resources on the client side to originate projects and increased competition—by multiples unheard of in recent past—on the provider side.

As a result, the tendency of many firms in dire need to generate revenue is to chase any request for qualifications or proposal, no matter how far afield from their core competency or serviceable geography. Worse, the chase proceeds with little or no insight or knowledge, let alone relationship with the client's decision makers. At what cost?

It would be one thing if the marketing effort to create a statement of qualifications or fee proposal and preparation of a conceptual solution was *free*. But it is not. Calculating your average *cost of goods sold*—to use manufacturing parlance—

would show that those costs can easily run into the tens of thousands, and often, on larger pursuits, hundreds of thousands of dollars.

The chances of actually winning new work are at best slim to none when:

1. You have no prior relationship with the client
2. You have no prior knowledge of the project
3. You have no experience with that type of project
4. You have no knowledge of the deliverable expectations, schedule, or budget
5. You have given no forethought to the availability or capability of internal resources (i.e., people) to first *win* the work—and then successfully *do* the work[6]

No matter how good you think your portfolio of experience is, it pales in the light of the relationships you have, or that the competition has likely already established. Put that same budget to client development and the results are markedly different.

---

[6] You can use those same five acknowledgements in your authenticity analysis to determine whether to pursue, or not, a particular project that will save you time and money! See Chapters 3 and 9 for more on this topic.

A series of industry surveys conducted in 1991, 1999, and 2009 questioned client behavior and service provider activities that happened before the RFP/Q was issued. The results showed that service providers who invested six to nine months of strategically orchestrated time to developing depth and breadth in the relationship with a client won the subsequent work an amazing 95-percent of the time![7]

More often than not, they understood the client's business better, knew the key client personnel on a personal level, and were in a position to lend honest, advisory expertise to help that client better craft the program for the project. They exemplified the *value* of their brand.

Invest your time and money in this approach and you will be winning more work and strengthening your brand!

---

[7] Lea, Bruce and J. Rossi, *What it Takes to Win (in Any Market): The Cold Hard Truth, SMPS Marketer*, December 2009, p. 7-10.

ON DISCOVERY

To build a successful brand, focus on the relationship between your service offerings and the needs of your clients. It is what you do every day that expresses your value and builds trust with your clients. The foundation of your brand is built by you and your staff by delivering on your mutual passion for your craft.

Bright Operations LLC

BRIGHT OPERATIONS: *The Trusted Advisor*

What if you have a long corporate history of successful strategic leadership and want to leverage your own personal brand to start your own firm?

This was the challenge faced by Ann Banning-Wright, president and founder of **Bright Operations,** a recent start-up management consultancy based in Los Angeles.

She founded Bright Operations in 2011 with a stated brand promise of "working with companies to accelerate growth," and a clever and appropriate tagline: *Step on it!* She started her own advisory business because saw a need to help time-starved CEOs and C-suite executives achieve greater success for their teams and their firms.

Ann came to the role of founder and CEO based on a long history and a solid personal brand as the first and only woman in senior leadership at Syska Hennessy Group. She was a non-engineer responsible for leading the strategic growth of one of the nation's largest engineering firms.

As senior vice president of the firm, her roles also included board member, chief strategy officer, and national director of strategic planning, marketing and communications, among other senior roles.

In Ann's words, she thrives on the possibility and potential of both individuals and teams, helping them realize where and what they can achieve and how to get there. Equally important, Ann inspires action and accountability to reach goals, leading to success and profits.

From personal experience, she understands the "front line" issues faced by firms navigating business and economic obstacles that stand in the way of their objectives, vision, and mission.

Ann believes that strategically harnessing this potential and promoting collaboration can push past the limitations of the status quo to take-action, resulting in firms becoming market leaders.

Ann's practice is based in Southern California, where she is active in many industry-related organizations and community programs that help keep her personal brand visible in the market she serves.

She exemplifies the thoughtful approach to leveraging her corporate experience to create a respected brand as a trusted advisor.

CHAPTER 2 | **Assessment**

Brand is the story that unites us in a common purpose and connects us with the people we serve.

MARK THOMSON

HOW ARE YOU PERCEIVED in the markets that you serve? You have probably heard, on more than one occasion, *"We already know what our clients think about us,"* only to find no direct correlation between this internal view and what clients actually say about your practice.

To determine the effectiveness of your brand image requires a determination of actual perception and an effort of honest reflection to gain real understanding.

PERCEPTION

A perception study goes right to the heart of your brand. What do your past, current, and potential clients think of your firm?

If your practice takes a primary role in projects, you should survey end-users and owners—both those responsible for hiring you, as well as those who use the spaces you create.

If you are a sub-consultant or subcontractor, you should survey both the prime companies who hire you and the end-users and owners who hire them. If the client can make a direct connection to the services for which you were responsible, you can gain valuable insight.

This effort should be market-centric (i.e., don't mix clients in healthcare with clients in higher education), but as geographically diverse as your practice. If done anonymously, it can include competitive analysis and client-perceived value questions. The sample set should be large. As with most surveys, you will get only a limited number of responses, but even with a small return, they will be representative.

What is the best way to survey? In-house or third party? In-person, phone, or electronic? It doesn't matter. Just do it; and do it often.

To ease the effort, use your existing relationships to create a "client satisfaction program." Invite your clients to participate at the outset of a project. Poll them periodically and briefly at the end of each phase of work. Do it again, six months after the project is complete. Build consistency into your survey program so you can track your progress over time.

Tom Boogher, executive vice president with environmental and testing engineers, PSI, concurs, *"We could debate the 'hows and whys' of client satisfaction surveys for hours—whether live or online, internal or external—but at the end of the day, I don't care how it is done as long as it gets done. Surveys are that important!"*

The traditional methods of tracking client perceptions are the best. If what you are tracking is only what's online, that can be a very small slice of the potential information.

Talking directly to the client, either through surveys or in person is best. Having a system in place and using it regularly is important. Direct outreach is not done often enough, but it is a competitive advantage for those firms that do.

Setting up a client satisfaction program provides a very simple way to engage your clients in a regular and ongoing dialogue. The improved and increased communication has several benefits.

A survey provides the client with the knowledge that you care enough to ask. It provides immediate feedback to your project team about how they are doing. It provides a venue to learn about potential future work. And, it allows you to measure increases or decreases in satisfaction over markets and time, which can flag organizational issues that are helping or hindering your progress.

Tracy Black, president of Black Cape Marketing, says, *"You can also use these surveys to better understand your market and your clients' needs. Find out what issues are keeping them up at night. Where do they think the market is headed? What changes do they see ahead? What are they doing organizationally to respond?"*

Black also notes that this insight will allow you to better position in the market. Some firms even go so far as to publish the results of this portion of their client surveys back out to the market as relevant benchmark data. This establishes them as both experts and business partners with clients and potential clients.

To gather the perception information you need, you can simply set up a series of short questions that align with the typical phases of your work; generally three to five for each phase.

Your survey should focus on key issues of collaboration and interaction:

- **Quality of communication**—*Are we listening?*
- **Adherence to schedule**—*Are we timely?*
- **Respect for budget limitations**—*Are we meeting your expectations?*

- **Trusted advice**—*Are we providing creative, innovative ideas that are making your project/business/users' lives better?*

- **Impact**—*Are we helping you achieve the results you need?*

Invite clients to participate by explaining how much you value their opinion and how their feedback will be incorporated into your organization. There is nothing better than allowing them to opt in. Define your schedule, approach, and expectations.

Simple online tools like Zoomerang and SurveyMonkey make the process of collecting data easier. More robust systems like Vovici provide serious metric evaluations.

There is nothing better than a phone call or meeting face to face. If you are concerned about getting honest and critical feedback, consider using a third party. A third party can either be someone inside your organization who is not directly involved in the work or an outside consultant that specializes in client feedback programs.

When survey data is collected at any stage of a project, make sure to report back to both your internal team and the client. When the project is complete, acknowledge your client's participation with thanks and possibly a small gift (e.g., a book or firm-branded item).

It can also be valuable to survey potential clients from time to time. Knowing how you are perceived by clients who haven't worked with you yet is important to understanding your brand image. Finding out why they hire your competition can be very insightful.

On the importance of survey client perceptions, Ann Banning-Wright, president of Bright Operations, notes, *"Firms are so self-absorbed and internally focused that they miss the opportunity to meet their clients' needs because they think their clients' needs are always the same. Your value is not what you did yesterday, your value is what you're going to do tomorrow to solve the untapped needs of your clients; and those needs are constantly changing."*

When it is all said and done: *"Ask and you shall receive."* It may not always be good news, but it will always be valuable information. Take it to heart and your people and projects will improve and your clients will thank you for that.

REFLECTION

Based on your self-discovery process of developing vision, mission, and values, and your review of client perceptions, the next step is to look in the mirror. If you have included staff representation from all levels within your organization in your business planning process, your strategic vision is more likely to resonate with everyone than if you have created a top-down mandate from the executive office.

So, the first step of assessment is to survey your staff to ascertain their view of your organization. Start with your values. Do they agree? Would they suggest others? Move to your mission; let them say *"what you do, for whom, how, and why, today."* Then get their opinion of your vision. Do they agree? Would they suggest otherwise?

Banning-Wright says, *"The clearer I can be with my brand, the more likely I will be to work with people who value results. My practice is about movement, action, and getting it done. The better I reflect what I value—a relentless focus on the client and bringing new challenges to satisfy them—the better I will be at building my brand."*

Black, adds, *"Be sure to survey as many people in your organization as possible. Let them know how valued their opinion is and how their input will be incorporated. Consider creating focus groups to get input from specific viewpoints within your organization."*

She also noted that new hires, for example, will have a fresh set of eyes on your organization. They will be able to tell you what values drew them to join your organization and give you feedback on whether or not they have found them to be as presented in the recruiting process.

Black says, *"New hires also have a recent perspective on competing firms that can be useful for benchmarking. Employees with longevity will have a perspective on the changes they have seen in your organization (both good and bad) and what values have maintained true and steady over time."*

Surveys can encompass other aspects of the practice including job satisfaction, management/employee relations, and opportunities for training and development. A regular employee survey program can be used to ensure that what you (actually they) are doing is aligned with your vision, mission, and values.

REALITY

Now compare. Comparing your client perceptions with your own self-assessment provides insight. When you have alignment between the external and internal views of your practice, you have a strong brand. If they are at odds, you have work to do.

The results of ongoing client-centric and staff-centric dialogue will allow you to continually assess how you are perceived.

When identity and image align, you can promote and position your firm for new work with the confidence that the market sees you in positive terms. When they do not align, you have to address the internal issues of how you practice, your processes, and your level of expertise in order to address external perceptions. What you don't want to hear is, "They are expensive, *and* they are slow!"

COMPARISONS

Preparing a simple comparison is a good first step. Using a common set of questions in both internal and external surveys enables a cross-comparison and evaluation. What are the *benefits* that define the *value* your firm provides to its clients? What are the four or five words you would use to describe how your firm delivers that value? What are the words your clients would use for those same questions?

The Architecture of Image

You can use this chart as an example to create your own brand assessment:

Issue	We Said	They Said
Process	Innovative	Reliable
Cost	Effective	Expensive
Breadth	Diverse	Specialized
Depth	Expert	Comparable
Reach	National	Regional

In the example above, this firm has some real issues of perception to address. If there are brand perception issues, they need to be addressed internally first.

Black notes, *"You cannot change how clients perceive you without changing how you perceive yourself."*

You may need a reality check where you think you are better than you are. Or, you may need to be more confident in areas where clients see more value in your service than you give yourselves. In either case, take the feedback seriously and use it to re-engineer your organization for positive change.

Webster's Musil agrees, *"To change perceptions, it is a relationship project. It takes one-on-one personal relationship marketing to make a change in perceptions. It takes more time than a marketing campaign, but in the end it is more effective."*

And after you make significant shifts, be sure to go back to your staff and clients and ask them again how you're doing in these same areas. Over time, you will be amazed at what you can accomplish toward an authentic brand.

ON ASSESSMENT

It is easy to think you know what your clients and your staff think about your service and your brand. You may have a clear understanding of your brand identity (the vision and mission that define our goals), but the reality is it is the client's perspective that defines your brand image. To understand your image requires the simple but sometimes painful, often rewarding act of just asking.

MULVANNY|G2
ARCHITECTURE

MulvannyG2 Architecture:
Value and Passion

MulvannyG2 Architecture, a 350-person design practice works internationally, focused on core markets that include retail stores, shopping centers, corporate office and interiors, and mixed-use buildings for brands of global significance. They are headquartered in Bellevue, Washington, and have offices in Portland, Oregon, Irvine, California, Washington, D.C., and Shanghai, China. Their vision statement and tagline is *"Shaping the Future Through Inspiring Design."*

Carla Thompson, global marketing director, says, *"We design buildings that help our clients build their brand. Whether it's a high rise or a large format retailer, we design a building to reflect their brand."*

MulvannyG2 resulted from a merger in 1999 between the Mulvanny Partnership, a commercial architecture practice that included five separate companies operating as divisions of Mulvanny, and Gerry Gerron's more design-oriented firm, G2 Architecture. Thompson comments, *"When Mulvanny merged with Gerry Gerron, the Mulvanny practice was best known for service and Gerry's practice was best known for design. Today, we use the strengths of both to enhance the entire practice."*

She acknowledged that the two firms had very different brands. Mulvanny was best known for their work with big-box retailer, Costco, where G2 was known for high-rise design and corporate architecture. The two firms consolidated to leverage the strengths of both brands and brought all the divisions under a single brand: MulvannyG2 Architecture.

The merged firms recognized the importance of quickly establishing the new brand. Thompson, noted, *"I was new to the firm and I saw an opportunity to strategize, design, and roll out a new consolidated branding program to coincide with the opening of our new corporate headquarters, which also played heavily into our brand building. We did it all in six months. It was intense, crazy, and fun."*

MulvannyG2 reinforces their vision and mission commitments with visual cues designed into all of their offices. Super-graphics, imprinted large on the walls of their lobby and throughout the office, convey their brand message to both staff and visitors.

Thompson, notes, *"One descriptive phrase we use a lot in both our environmental graphics and our collateral is 'Design at Work.' The tagline is intended to reflect our 'roll-up-our-sleeves-and-get-things-done' work ethic and service orientation, as much as our commitment to our clients to design facilities that improve their bottom line—whether it be by selling more merchandise, getting higher lease rates, or helping employees be more productive."*

She shared that in their lobbies they have big, inspirational graphics, with words like *"excellence defined in everything we do,"* *"learn and grow,"* and *"embrace change."* They use these metaphors as motivators for their staff and as a brand promise to their clients to confirm their commitment to design, practice, and service excellence.

Thompson adds, *"We use key words to give shape to what excellence means to the firm. We use these same messages in all of our offices to convey that this is not just another architectural firm, but one that is focused on the client experience."*

Similarly, MulvannyG2 emphasizes its core values based on the acronym 'PACE' for profitability, accountability, clarity, and excellence. Their strategic plan has cascading goals associated with each of those, starting with firm-wide goals that trickle down to office, market sector, and individual goals.

Thompson acknowledges that tracking brand impact is important. They monitor the public relations impact of everything they send, publish, or post on social media sites. They also use social media to follow their clients and key press relationships. Their goal is to project a corporate culture that is design oriented, philanthropic, and fun.

Thompson shared that they recently unveiled a new internal brand identity campaign called WOW! There are posters throughout their offices that proclaim "WOW Someone Today!" to solicit nominations from leadership and staff. The program focuses on celebrating what their people are doing to go above and beyond, by improving themselves, the firm, or their clients' business. They will use the program to show examples of best practices throughout the firm.

The firm publishes two bi-monthly e-newsletters, *Rethink Architecture* and *Design at Work*. The first explores what they are doing differently to rethink the business of architecture to benefit clients and communities. On alternating months, the second features a bulletin board format with post-it notes and pinned pictures that link to interviews with clients and potential clients who share their perspective on what is important in in their world, as well as market trends, YouTube videos, and company news. Both e-newsletters have won first place awards in SMPS' Marketing Communications Awards program.

The firm also creates very specialized brochures and proposals branded around the client. Thompson notes, *"It is important to remember with any marketing collateral—the message is all about them."*

As part of their marketing efforts, they do a lot of field research. Thompson shared, *"We were pursing an opportunity to develop a new prototype for an established retailer. We sent about 35 of our* *staff from around the country, armed with $50 gift cards, to do 'man-on-the-street' research on their experience with the retailer's stores. As a result of experiencing the entrance and wayfinding in their existing stores and interacting with their sales staff, we prepared an unsolicited research report. That extra effort changed their perception of our firm and won the project."*

Thompson noted that doing things the same way will not take MulvannyG2 to the next level. They continually ask themselves what they can do to bring more value. *"In large architectural firms, design is a given. We recognize that raising the bar on the client experience is the key to differentiation."*

Thompson acknowledges, *"While we are best known as dependable, hard-working, and trustworthy, according to client perception studies, our brand image is always a work in progress. As we add people and new clients, our brand evolves to reflect the design work we do and who we work for."*

The Architecture of Image

CHAPTER 3 | **Authenticity**

> ### *It is not slickness, polish, or cleverness that makes a brand a brand. It is truth.*
>
> HARRY BECKWITH

LET'S ASSUME FOR THE MOMENT that through the discovery and assessment reviews, you determine that your brand alignment between internal and external perceptions is very strong.

How do you maintain a strong brand? That comes from the *consistent* delivery of your service—the practice of your practice—and the progression your practice makes to meet the changing needs and demands of your markets.

ALIGNMENT

Ralph Waldo Emerson once said, referring to governmental bureaucrats, *"Foolish consistency is the hobgoblin of little minds."* However, in professional service, operational consistency is often the hallmark of a strong brand. Industry-respected measures like ISO 9000[8] and Lean Six Sigma[9] illustrate that brand value can be reflected by consistent process. Both of these internationally accepted certification programs focus on quality and measurable and repeatable processes as the foundation for a high-value brand.

However, don't let your standard processes get in the way of innovation and creative delivery of unexpected results. *"The way we have always done it"* is too often the excuse for lack of innovation.

EXPERTISE

Expertise creates the opportunity for professionals to build the *right practice* that is designed around your vision, mission, enduring principles, and strategic goals.

On-going professional development at all levels of your practice is critical to maintaining a strong brand. Does your firm have leadership, continuing education, or professional development programs? Does it leverage the input from "outside" expertise and a rigorous learning-oriented program?

---

[8] The ISO 9000 standards are related to quality management systems and designed to help organizations ensure that they meet the needs of customers and other stakeholders.

[9] Lean Six Sigma is a synergized managerial concept of Lean and Six Sigma that results in the elimination of wastes in the provision of service.

Or does it rely on aging internal training modules, or worse, from the biased input of only attending vendor-oriented lunch-and-learn programs designed to provide easy continuing education credits?

Lippincott's Wilke, notes, *"The alignment of the culture and the values of each company coming together is as important as resolving the name and identity."*

PROGRESSION

Market dynamics change the expectations for your practice. Only a very few years ago, sustainable design and building information modeling (BIM) were considered differentiators for firms in the building industry. Today, delivering a green-certified, building-information-modeled design is the basic cost of entry, in the construction market.

Constant evaluation of client expectations, using the same type of satisfaction survey system described earlier, can give insight into developing trends that will influence their need for your services and help you create internal development programs to keep your staff at the forefront.

The Architecture of Image

The idea of an integral, holistic approach is fundamental to the premise of branding your professional practice. A focus on value creation, leveraging expertise, excellence, and experience is the key.

PURSUIT

One of the clearest measures of authenticity is taking an honest look at your rationale for any given opportunity pursuit. Being informed and targeted can be the difference between winning and losing business. Being honest about your ability to succeed can save time and money better spent on building stronger relationships and brand awareness than on a wishful or spurious pursuit.

Maximizing your marketing resources to achieve results has never been more important than today. An informed strategy, good decision-making, and efficient processes can increase return for investment in a challenging economy. The key to driving a ubiquitous marketing culture can come in the form of a strategic go/no-go decision-making process. [10]

---

[10] Black, Tracy, *Drive Strategic Marketing Culture*, Zweig-White Marketing Now, April 2010, p11.

When you sharpen your business strategy and implement a more rigorous structure of authenticity for your pursuits you can avoid common "cultural loopholes" that can undermine your brand.

Tracy Black observes, *"When your leadership or staff finds ways to justify a pursuit without much real thought to the implications of time, resources, and cost, it is a recipe for wasted time and effort."*

An authenticity-based pursuit process supports the brand-oriented culture you are trying to build. Even in a robust economy, a shotgun approach to pursuing projects does not build brand value.

To develop a more strategic marketing culture, look for patterns of past success. Then examine your existing pursuit process along with industry best practices. This will help create a vision for what your ideal process could look like.

SMPS's Worth says, *"Customer relationship management systems have given firms a better understanding of client needs, of how they look at service providers, and the way they look at future projects. By setting up a series of checkpoints—so that a project pursuit does not move forward unless all the indicators point forward—gets everyone engaged in the pursuit process. Otherwise you may be wasting time and energy on a pursuit that does not align with your brand."*

Next, craft the components of an authentic pursuit strategy. There are three basic categories that need to be evaluated:

- **Your relationship to the client**
- **Your experience and expertise related to the project**
- **The capabilities of the competition and their relationship with the client**

In each category, identify the specific criteria that you know will determine success for your firm. Then customize, prioritize, and weight the criteria.

Black recommends, *"You may choose to categorize clients as existing, high potential, or future potential. In this case, the first item on your form assigns a value based on those three categories (10, nine, or eight points, respectively) and zero points for a client with little or no established relationship."*

Black also notes, *"You can see how weighting the points can dramatically affect the scoring—if the client hasn't been on your radar screen, it's pretty hard to make up nine or more points."*

Black added that having an established relationship with the client is the most important factor for success. However, it can also be the place where you find the most loopholes. So give it the most points and no room for interpretation.

As a bonus, by incorporating client category definitions, you can culturally reinforce the processes of both pursuit and vertical market classification.

Look for other criteria that support the cultural changes you want to make. For example, to minimize last-minute decisions that keep the marketing staff up past midnight and result in poor-quality proposals, incorporate criteria for how early you learn about the RFQ/P, how much time you have to respond, and whether or not the right people are available to put together a quality proposal. Points add up or subtract quickly.

Black reiterates, *"To promote a more collaborative approach to support organizational changes driven by your strategic plan, add check points to make sure the right people are involved in evaluating every pursuit."*

Looking beyond the pursuit analysis process, this same approach can improve your proposals and presentations. For example, to help develop compelling strategies that address a client's issues in the proposal and minimize boilerplate, add required fields for the client's hot buttons and your relevant differentiators.

Those answers can be transferred directly onto your proposal and presentation process to reinforce strategy and messaging consistently throughout the pursuit.

Black adds, *"In the end, your pursuit process will have criteria and categories and the weighted scores that equal 100 for a perfect pursuit. Using a spreadsheet simplifies the calculation of points and can assign a traditional letter grade (A+ down to F), to facilitate discussion."*

Further, by requiring increasingly higher levels of approval in inverse order of the score allows lower scores to be considered for strategic reasons, but only with buy-in from key leaders.

This process will provide honest rationale for not pursuing a particular opportunity, but can also provide justification for pursuing a project with a low score, because it provides an entrée building a relationship with a target client.. This way you won't create a form that dictates an answer, but rather a tool that encourages strategic, collaborative decision making.

Rolling out a new form is less painful when it aligns with your brand goals, your strategic plan, and supports the cultural behaviors you are encouraging across the organization.

Black says, *"A few employees will always cringe at a new process, but once they see how easily it supports authenticity of brand, good decision-making and increased return on investment, it can quickly become an accepted practice."*

She reinforces the importance of strategic pursuit strategies, adding, *"Remember, in a tough economy: no shotguns, and no loopholes."*

The old adage *"If it seems too good to be true, it probably is"* is an excellent portent when someone suggests pursuing a project with a very high potential fee, but no real basis or probability for winning the pursuit.

Honest analysis of the risk and reward of chasing the proverbial *"project of a lifetime"* can lead to better investment of time and effort toward "clients for a lifetime" and a stronger brand.

IT IS WHAT IT ISN'T

It is what it is! You seem to hear this aphorism everywhere you turn these days. Does this contemporary catch-phrase represent acceptance or resignation for the authenticity of your brand? Does it reflect wisdom or ignorance?

The economic realities of the latest post-recession period mean less potential work, more competition, and lack of loyalty from long-held clients. This is due to the same business-to-business pressures and numerous critical issues facing operations, administration, and business development within your firm, as well as that of your clients.

These overarching concerns can cause even the most experienced professional to speak in terms of indifference to outcomes they can't seem to control.

However, one of the hallmarks of the authentic brand is the ability to think creatively, neither in nor outside the box, but with a *"what box?"* mindset. There is no good reason to accept "it is what it is," unless you don't have the time or will to affect change.

The challenge is one that requires discipline, focus, and a willingness to suspend negative influences. The key is to look for a solution that embraces all of the elements of a what-if scenario with the perspective of potential and possibility.

Envisioning a positive outcome and defining strategies and programs to achieve that goal is fundamental to having a brand that is perceived as authentic. After all, clients hire you to provide creative solutions, not just the same-old, same-old output.

Accepting *"it is what it is"* is a cop-out. So, the next time you start to say it, stop and take a day to explore options. See if you can't come up with an idea that allows you to say, *"Here's what it could be!"* Doing any less is inauthentic. Optimism delivered enhances your brand.

ON AUTHENTICITY

Aligning your expertise with your client's need for your service reinforces an authentic approach to the market and to creating a strong brand. Being all things to all clients rarely provides the quality of service they expect, and ultimately diminishes brand value. Today, the affirmation *"to thine own self be true"* has never been truer. Your client will value your honesty and see an authentic brand.

B N I M

BNIM: *Walking Their Talk*

An excellent example of a firm that exemplifies their vision, mission, and values every day is the architecture firm known as **BNIM**. Principal and founding partner, Steve McDowell, FAIA, likes to say to their clients, *"No one knows as much as everyone."* This phrase is a hallmark for a firm that differentiates its design approach as collaborative, holistic, and open.

BNIM is an architecture and design firm founded in 1970 as Berkebile, Nelson, Immenschuh, & McDowell. The firm went through a rebranding effort in 2010 and compressed its name to the acronym BNIM to reflect how the firm was best known in the market. Headquartered in Kansas City, Missouri, the firm has offices in Houston, Texas; Des Moines, Iowa; and and San Diego, California. BNIM has nearly 100 design professionals and support staff.

The firm's brand identity is that of an innovative leader in designing high-performance environments. Through an integrated process of collaborative discovery, they create transformative, living design that leads to vital and healthy organizations and communities.

The Architecture of Image

BNIM is a national leader in design excellence, sustainable design, practice, and technology. The American Institute of Architects (AIA) recognized BNIM with the *2011 AIA Architecture Firm Award*, the highest honor bestowed for consistently producing distinguished architecture.

BNIM was celebrated for advancing the design of sustainable architecture from nearly its inception to today, as it has become a preeminent force fundamentally re-shaping the built environment.

As early pioneers in the arena of sustainable design, BNIM's process is deeply rooted in the concept of integration, where clients and collaborators work together to create buildings and spaces that embrace the triple bottom line—a balance of people, planet and prosperity.

Maria Maffry, vice president of business development, says, *"BNIM's brand is truly about making the world a better place. It goes beyond just buildings to touch the human element and really make a difference for people and communities."*

BNIM has a diverse practice providing architecture, interior design, planning, and landscape design and the firm is nationally known for leadership in sustainable design and the future of post-carbon economy.

BNIM shares its values with its employees and its clients, and defines them as follows:

- We seek a better way.
- We are committed to long-term thinking and measurable improvement as a way of life in every community we touch.
- We seek to increase the vitality of people, planet, and prosperity equally.
- We are passionate about generous design, believing that it inspires people and changes the world for the better.
- We insist on being excellent—in execution, performance, and results.
- We care about what our buildings do and how they positively impact the lives of people, organizations, and communities.
- We operate with a spirit of authenticity and servant leadership.
- We embrace diversity in our culture—in perspective, voice, and skills.
- We promote integrated thinking and a collaborative dialog of discovery.
- We partner to find the answers.
- We embrace the challenge of innovation and the advantage of replication.

These enduring principles set the brand standard that BNIM strives to deliver every day. Their focus on values is the hallmark of a strong brand.

PART II
COLLABORATION | Your Brand *Builds*

Treat people as if they were what they ought to be and you'll
help them to become what they are capable of becoming.
JOHANN WOLFGANG VON GOETHE

PROFESSIONAL SERVICE IS A COLLABORATIVE EFFORT. The building
industry relies on collaboration between designers, engineers,
contractors, and owners. Students coming into the workforce
come from collaborative, team-based learning environments.
Industries in virtually every market require collaboration
between suppliers, distributers, and service providers to deliver
value to their clients and customers.

For your brand to build to grow and endure, your practice must
focus on collaboration as part of its ongoing development and
brand extension and the many types of transformation that
occur as markets mature and evolve.

LEADERSHIP

One of the most effective brand builders is developing and promoting leadership within your practice. Leadership can manifest in different ways and can benefit the firm and individuals.

There are several types of leadership that occur within any professional service firm:

- **Firm leadership**—establishing vision and management best practices that result in significant and sustained, profitable growth

- **Market leadership**—being ranked in the industry press for size, revenue, or results

- **Technical leadership**—being recognized for expertise and innovation

All have the capacity to provide third-party validation of your efforts—one of the most powerful tools in creating brand value recognition with new prospective clients.

Management expertise—the ability to demonstrate unique, differentiating, and profitable operational methods that have helped your firm succeed—can be shared through press interviews, association awards programs, and other business-to-business roundtables.

The willingness to reveal what you have tried—what has worked and what has failed—to an audience of your clients and peers is usually viewed as strength of character, and by association, brand strength as well. A few may fear giving away secrets, but in reality there are few secrets, only aspirations that have been tried, failed, and not tried for fear of failure. True leaders do not fear revealing the methods of their success.

Market leadership is a function of metrics and measures. It requires discipline that documents results in ways that can be used to grade progress or decline, which should be fundamental to the practice. Metric barometers (See Chapter 9 for more) are part of a dashboard of data that, in the best case, provide forward-looking trend analysis to help leaders guide the firm.

These same metrics are judged by industry journals as a way to rank firm position nationally and, increasingly, globally. Whether annual revenue, sales, numbers of deals/projects, value of projects, or staff size, these rankings provide a method of establishing preeminence in your field of practice. Local, regional, and national rankings can be used to promote leading firms, and give lesser-ranked firms a target for which to shoot.

The Architecture of Image

Developing and positioning outward-facing technical experts is an excellent way to build sustainable firm leaders. By championing the benefit of industry expertise and innovation, you and your staff can express passion for the practice of the practice, at general to granular levels. Older staff can speak from wisdom and perspective, while younger staff can speak from opportunity and potential.

Both speaking and publishing provide venues for expression of individual expertise through public forums that add credibility and validation to your ideas. Industry press are always seeking content and cultivating relationships with editors and reporters can lead to greater visibility.

Participation *behind the lectern* at industry and client-facing associations, conferences, and seminars provides an outlet for persuasive demonstration of ideas and dialogue on issues facing your clients and your peers.

Each of these approaches builds confidence and credibility that can be promoted to existing and prospective clients. And each approach builds self-confidence and commitment to the practice, which is the foundation for sustainable leadership.

STRATEGY

Your strategy, like the structure of a building, organizes your vision, mission, values, and goals into a framework that allows you to deliver on your brand promise.

Collaboration plays a critical role in shaping your brand. Your collaborative processes define how your service is delivered and control the quality of the experience. These structures, and the decisions about how they are established, enforced, and evolve, are the cornerstones to your brand.

The leadership models you employ set the stage for the quality of the output of your service. If these models can be replicated, you have the opportunity to branch out into new geographies or to grow vertically on the strength of the underlying framework.

The role of the professional service firm is to provide advisory knowledge to benefit a client's interests or issues. The challenge each firm faces is balancing their efforts between multiple clients—needed to maintain and grow the practice—and to serve them all with equal energy and focus.

The Architecture of Image

The marketer's role is to help prioritize the identification, pursuit, and acquisition of new clients consistent with the strategic growth goals and operational abilities of the firm to serve them.

Collaboration between marketing and operational leadership ensures that growth strategies focus on winning new work with clients whose needs align with the capability of the service firm to excel at providing solutions.

In a challenging economy—marked by fewer potential opportunities and increased competition—marketing strategies must focus on building and winning work within your firm's *sweet spot* and not be lured into wasting energy on low-probability pursuits.

At the same time, operational focus must ensure that equal and excellent effort is put forward to meet existing obligations for all current clients, regardless of size or stature. Every client deserves your best. Regardless of size or scope, the result of right practice pays dividends.

ON COLLABORATION

Referrals and references, kudos and awards, and repeat business and extended engagements result from delivering exemplary collaborative service to each client, based on their goals and objectives and your ability to deliver the desired service.

This combination of strategic focus and operational excellence is the hallmark of the successful professional service firm and the foundation of a strong and enduring brand. Those who learn to collaborate in this environment can succeed beyond expectation.

CHAPTER 4 | Acumen

Creativity can solve almost any problem. The creative act—the defeat of habit by originality—overcomes everything.

GEORGE LOIS

THE ONGOING DEVELOPMENT of any professional service brand requires a continual review and adjustment of the intelligence that you bring to the marketplace.

This acumen comes internally and from your network of collaborators. It is the insight that you gain from working with your clients and how you share that information with the market.

Next to quality of service delivery, one of the most important parts of a professional service firm's brand is its expertise and how that thought leadership is positioned and shared in the marketplace.

No other non-operational marketing factor—not advertising, social media, or a beautiful website—trumps the impact of having an expert write in a client-centric publication or speak at a client-facing seminar or conference.

Geotechnologies' Mike Savage notes, *"It starts as you develop a knowledge-base about a client, or client type. Your brand value becomes exponential when they know you know so much about them. You become a resource library of information. As you build trust you become more entrenched. As you deliver on your promise and don't get greedy, you won't force them to make you compete on price."*

HGA's Luers concurs, *"Brand is important, but everyone struggles with it. We work hard to attain a higher level of awareness both internally and externally with a focus on unified message and a national marketing strategy. We emphasize message consistency. And, we benchmark against competitors."*

SMPS' Worth says, *"If you have a key person who can be positioned as a thought leader—sharing with the industry through dialogue about new methods or technologies—you can make a real difference. That thought leadership can be demonstrated on the Internet or by presenting at conferences or seminars."*

INTELLIGENCE

Your business strategy defines how you promote your brand identity—what you offer, where you practice, what makes you different, and how you provide value. As with any effort for continual improvement, your strategy must evolve as your market matures.

PSI's Boogher adds, *"As a differentiator, we have some proprietary systems that drive how we deliver our information. However, like many firms in our industry, we hire bright people, with the right degrees and licenses and the right experience, so that on an expertise level, we're all pretty much the same—and in the clients' mind, often somewhat interchangeable. I believe your differentiators are earned by your service and how you interact with and touch your clients. It is their experience that differentiates you from the competition, which is more important than technical skills."*

By going beyond your expertise to address the core issues facing your clients, your clients' clients, and your communities, you can create collaborative processes that make your clients' world a better place to achieve *their* mission and vision.

MulvannyG2's Thompson says, *"It comes down to people. The best way to differentiate is to focus on your people's experience, expertise, and personality because clients hire people. They fire firms."*

You can do this by hiring industry experts, such as school superintendents and campus planners for education, hospital executives for healthcare, funding and finance specialists for both public and private development, and leaders from other market sectors who bring unique and relevant perspectives to inspire innovation.

Your firm can create an advisory board of clients from common or different vertical markets to participate in regular, annual or semi-annual, facilitated discussions of trends. This type of investment can yield untapped needs that your firm can expand on and deliver.

This outside advisory approach can be expanded to include non-competitor service providers, contractors and integrators, and vendors to give additional, and often unexpected, perspective.

INSIGHT

Insight is the brand value that you share with the market to produce a result not obtainable by any other firm. Developing thought leaders and thought leadership in a particular market or service area allows you to be seen as bringing higher value. Professional service providers have passion for their work—tap into that passion and you can turn a practitioner into a true professional.

Identify client-facing outlets in print, web, or at conferences and support your technical staff to get involved. Help them become comfortable with writing and speaking. Being known as thought leaders takes your brand to the pinnacle of perception.

BNIM's Maffry comments, *"Our brand is both who we are and also projects what we aspire to be through core values that inform each action and project decision. It's not static. Our brand is where we want to go and not just where we've been. Even though our brand is evolving, there is a core that is consistent and aligned between the existing and new. We know our clients seek us for who we are and the innovation and forward-thinking that we provide."*

For firms that have the inclination to research, applying and sharing lessons learned with their clients, is an important part of their brand. Explore those opportunities first, but know they are different for every firm.

Luers says, *"We try hard to do measureable research that's not just post-occupancy, but also looks at the changes impacting our client's industries. We use that information to create new tools and share our thinking about the future, not just about designing a project today."*

In this era of "big data," professional service firms—and particularly their marketers and business developers—rely primarily on facts and statistics to convey their value proposition.

There is nothing more scintillating to a client than hearing that a firm is "more than 100 years old," has "20 (or more) offices," has "500 licensed engineers," or has constructed "more than 1 million square feet" of new buildings in the last 10 years. Oh, and by the way, we are "always" on time and on budget.

Just kidding!

Too often, these mind-numbing, eye-glazing factoids have replaced real narrative about the challenge, approach, solution, and benefits as proof of the ability of the firm to provide real and sustainable value for their clients.

Why? Facts are simple to remember and to regurgitate. For the non-technical marketing and business developer, facts are the easy answer. Writing value-based narrative is increasingly a lost art. And, again too often, the original storytellers—those involved in the development and delivery of the service—are gone or weren't asked.

Today, there is such a focus on the structure and the data contained in customer relationship management (CRM) systems as the be-all end-all resource for knowledge that the stories have gotten lost in the database. The rise of visual media (i.e., television, its Internet cohorts like NetFlix, HuLu, VuDu, etc.) and instant, social media communication (i.e., Twitter, LinkedIn, Facebook, and on, and on...) has had a noticeable impact on both the narrator and the narrative.

To return to effective storytelling and communication—whether marketer or business developer or technical professional—you must engage with the consultants, designers, engineers, project managers, and clients involved in each project at the outset.

The Architecture of Image

Start a dialogue, document the progress, and create a story worth telling and hearing. Nothing supports and validates brand value like a good story.

Chris Watson, national director of marketing at Gilbane Building Company, notes, *"Positioning through speaking is an important part of our outreach efforts. We focus on speaking opportunities at every trade show we attend. We submit applications to industry-related shows—40 to 50 engagements a year. When we are able to get on a panel or present with a client, it is a great way for people to see how we interact. We use the opportunity to promote the success of our clients. This makes it much easier to position for the next project."*

Luers concurs, *"It is important to educate the market. By speaking at client conferences, we can share primary research. Our staff has become much more supportive of this branding effort. Our staff is encouraged to write and speak. In the past, it was a little like pulling teeth. Now we submit presentation prospectuses eight to ten times a year and author white papers that we post on our website, LinkedIn, and Facebook."*

Thompson agrees, *"We try to get our people speaking as often as possible. We have at least 30 conferences on the calendar where we submit presentation ideas to get our people positioned as experts."*

Worth, adds, *"One of the best ways to build brand recognition for your firm comes through participation in outside organizations. The very best way to become more visible is to become active in their process. Get involved."*

FROM THOUGHT TO PRINT TO PODIUM

Several years ago, I had the opportunity to interview marketing expert and author of more than a dozen books, Seth Godin for a cover article for the SMPS journal, *Marketer.* Having done several interviews in the past—using a preset list of questions, taking copious notes, and relying on my memory to flush out the article—I called to set up a time for us to talk, suggesting I'd need about an hour. Godin called back and suggested I tape our interview, have it transcribed, and then edit the draft conversation into the article.

Godin's comment was, *"If I gave you an hour, we'd have another book."* He noted that a typical 30-minute interview, where he spoke freely on a topic where he was passionately and intellectually expert, would generate 3,000 to 4,000 words. As a typical magazine or journal article is 1,000 to 1,500 words, I would have plenty of raw materials to draw from. While actually not quite another book, he was right about the volume of content.

I've used that simple method ever since to help turn technical staff within my firm—who are reticent about writing for publication—into respected *experts*, who were then sought after for their knowledge by other publications. And, by extension, gave those same individuals the confidence to present that same content as part of a client-facing industry trade conference.

INNOVATION

Client organizations go through the same evolution as the service firm—driven by evolving market demands that can set the stage for innovation. Research by your experts on trends related to their area of knowledge can yield areas underserved or not served at all.

Innovation is the application of creativity. It takes a good idea and turns it into a market driver. Fostering a culture of innovation—an *idea factory,* if you will—can fuel the continual growth of your firm and your brand.

Creativity and innovation is the life blood of the branding effort. Without skillful ideation, every firm would look like every other firm—the death knell of a brand.

An innovative marketing process can be applied to the branding effort by creating a new message, establishing or sustaining a position in the market, or simply identifying possibilities for new services.

This innovation process can be defined in six phases.

1. **Considering the Possibilities**
   Engage regularly in a freewheeling, no-holds-barred, no-wrong-answers, brainstorming, "idea factory" meeting. Set a strategic premise (what is your goal) and then let the creativity begin. Without exception there will be some good, some bad, and some "what-if-we-could..." ideas. Avoid setting implicit or implied limits (e.g., don't stop at "going global" when you could be "going galactic"), and definitely don't raise judgments or doubts about anyone's suggestion. Inspiration and innovation often come from the least likely idea. Don't be afraid to look outside your normal spheres of influence. Check out the competition; better check out your clients. A marketing message that resonates is driven by benefits and value.

2. **Freeform Associative Cognition**

    Spend some time prioritizing (but don't throw any ideas away). Focus on three good ideas that meet your strategic goal and expand on them. What is their message? How would they be seen or experienced by the customer? How will they be extended into other aspects of your practice? How are they expressed (i.e., what medium and media)? As in Step 1, there are no wrong answers—all ideas are good ideas. Look back at the early ideas (that didn't move forward) and see if any expand, complement, or improve the ones you are studying.

3. **Discipline and Focus**

    Pick one! This is the hardest step, since you probably have many good ideas to choose from. Take that "really" good idea and think through all the options to take it from concept to fruition, from inspiration to execution. What resources are needed? What budget? How quickly can you go to market? This is the time to set out a plan that moves the idea forward. Most plans can be developed in just a few hours, no more than a few days, and none should span more than six weeks. Setting an aggressive schedule keeps the focus on the goal and keeps the idea fresh.

4. **Effecting a Solution**

    This is where the rubber meets the road! Buddha said, *"An idea that is developed and put into action is more important than an idea that only exists as an idea."* However your idea manifests—as a new service or piece of collateral or e-marketing; a move into new market; or an event or promotional effort—this is the time to follow through by making it visible. This is where the idea is translated into form, where you show it to the world, and where it builds your brand.

5. **Retrospection**

   Take a breath. Sleep on it. Don't worry. And definitely, don't second guess yourself. Many good (and even great) ideas go to market and don't realize the impact that targeted. Conversely, many do make a difference, set a new high-water mark for the brand, become iconic, and remain memorable. And many great ideas morph into new ideas that take that initial creativity and expand into even greater innovation.

6. **Happy Feet!**

   Smile. You have developed a new program that will help build and extend your brand, built on the six phases of the creative act, and will be ready to go back to number one and start again.

ON ACUMEN

Expert knowledge is the basis for professional service. Investing in continuing education, research, and personnel (and personal) development and the promotion of thought leadership within your field is one of the most important aspects of building and sustaining a notable brand.

Those firms that tread water by being *just one in the crowd* will rarely survive in the marketplace. Those that stand up and make a statement, share wisdom, and collaborate freely to discover new methods and innovative solutions will endure.

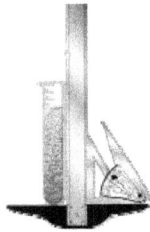

GEOTECHNOLOGIES: *The Personal Network*

When you are a smaller fish in a larger pond, leveraging the firm's history can be a differentiator, but being visible in the industry's network makes the real difference.

Geotechnologies, Inc. exemplifies the power of longevity and planned transition with a consistent and highly visible contribution to their network.

Geotechnologies provides specialized services in the areas of geotechnical design, geotechnical consulting, and geotechnical testing and monitoring in the greater Southern California market. As a small firm with a staff of 22, the firm competes with many larger firms.

The firm has gone through three major brand initiatives in its 40-year history. Founded in 1971, as Geology and Soils Consultants, two years later the firm adopted the names of its founding partners and became known, like many designers and engineers, by their names—first, as Kovacs-Byer and Associates and then in 1992 as Jerry Kovacs & Associates.

The Architecture of Image

In 2000, when the remaining founder retired, the next generation of owners, Mike Savage and Ed Hill, rebranded the firm under its current name, Geotechnologies, Inc.

According to Savage, throughout the firm's history it has had the same mission—to serve their clients in the building industry with responsive engineering and testing services.

The firm provides geotechnical and geology survey, analysis, and testing services to owners, owner's reps, and developers for projects in education—K-12, college and university—and other public work projects for Cities and Counties in the region.

As a testament to their reputation in the market, Geotechnologies has consulted on more than 20,000 projects in Southern California.

For a small firm, understanding the concept of brand value is critical. Savage noted that to continue building business and maintaining existing relationships, their brand is intrinsic to their discipline.

In defining their values, Geotechnologies is committed to quality, teamwork, and responsiveness. What is notable about the firm's brand is how their professional staff develops and maintains strong relationships with clients, local agencies, and other industry professionals.

To compete with the larger competitors, Geotechnologies maintains a very high level of visibility through active participation in professional associations, client event sponsorship, and a commitment to providing value to their network. They focus on "marquee" client-benefit events that typically draw from the broadest sectors of the business community.

Savage is known locally and regionally as a "connector," someone you can go to for an introduction to someone you need to know.

Savage's advice: *"Spend a lot of time speaking to others in the industry who might not directly hire you. You don't know who knows whom, and you never know where a lead might come from. Everybody knows somebody you want to know. You may have your targets at an event, but you continue to connect with people."*

He definitely knows, and is known by, his network and, as a result, continually builds Geotechnologies' brand.

CHAPTER 5 | Maturity

You have to do stuff that average people don't understand,
because those are the only good things.
ANDY WARHOL

THE EXPERTISE THAT IS THE FOUNDATION for your practice
continually evolves as new tools, methods, and materials
become available and inform the solutions you deliver. These
same new ideas and functions influence your brand.

EXPANSION

As firms realize success, there is a natural tendency to grow
geographically. Existing clients can take you to new locales.
Similar clients can draw you, knowing you successfully serve
customers like them. Your research may find geographic areas
underserved by your service. The simple fact of opening a new
office is a brand advantage. It adds breadth to your depth.

Organic growth is a good way to expand your brand. That said,
there are almost always provincial prejudices that work against
the outsider. This challenge can be best met through the same

positioning and awareness processes that you used in your home town.

Connecting your local leaders with the new community's network of potential clients, peer service providers, and vendors builds awareness. Focusing on being seen as an expert through interviews in the local business press, participation in chamber of commerce and other business organizations, and presenting at local/regional luncheons, seminars, and conferences, can all build positive brand perceptions.

Organic expansion is the lowest cost method of growing your brand. It takes a little longer than acquisition, but buying your way in comes with its own set of challenges.

When you grow through acquisition, you buy the opportunity to quickly expand your brand. A local, like, service provider will already have some level of brand recognition. However, before you buy, it is always advisable to survey just how positive (or negative) the existing brand actually is.

The goodwill from a positive brand can go a long way to quickly expanding your practice and improving your brand. In accounting parlance, goodwill is the value of an asset owned that is intangible, but has a quantifiable "prudent value" in a business. For example, the reputation the firm enjoyed with its clients has a calculable goodwill value. A poor reputation can negatively impact both the acquisition cost and the longer-term brand potential.

Evaluating another firm for merger or acquisition potential requires the same discovery and assessment process as you have done for measuring your own brand value. Anything less is a recipe for trouble.

EXTENSION

While the easiest thing to sell is the same service to the same client, the hardest is selling new services to new clients. That challenge, while daunting, is another factor in extending your brand. Developing new service offerings can challenge your practice to be innovative, which in turn helps differentiate you from your competition.

As an example, several years ago—and at the very beginning of the green-building movement—architects and engineers Fields Devereaux (now Harley Ellis Devereaux), an established California regional design/engineering firm, recognized the emerging trend toward sustainable design. The firm's leadership created a separately branded sustainability design and commissioning subsidiary practice called GreenWorks Studio. As one of the first to market, GreenWorks now successfully provides its services to corporate and institutional clients, regardless of who the client uses for architectural design.

Brand extension works best when the new service has some connection to an existing service offering. As The Sextant Group, a national audiovisual and acoustical consultancy, began its strategic growth initiative, Mark Valenti, the founder, acquired a lighting design firm, while at the same time adding accredited information technology/telecommunications and security systems design staff.

This nearly doubling of their technology service offerings and staff allowed the firm to grow even during a slowing economy, while at the same time increasing brand equity by improving the depth and breadth of technical services the firm could offer. In recent years, the firm also added a technology-savvy educator who works with their higher education clients, facilitating faculty development with new pedagogies, which further distinguishes their brand in the market.

Whether you create a self-standing organization that develops a unique brand message or extend an existing brand by adding complementary services, brand extension is a natural growth initiative. However, that same growth through extension can have a negative impact on your brand if you determine to offer services not directly or even indirectly associated with your core competencies.

For example, a firm best known for designing corporate office space decided, due to the downturn in the economy, to try their hand in design for a more active market in religious facilities. The resultant distraction of positioning and pursuit into a market where they had no expertise or experience had the effect of diluting their marketing efforts in their primary sector. This effort was also viewed as opportunistic and inauthentic by the clients in the worship space market.

Grow based on your strengths. Don't get distracted by apparent low-hanging fruit that may not be quite ripe for you. There comes a time when your brand can and should be extended. This can come from the natural evolution of the practice of the practice to grow geographically, or from creating something "brand" new! Pun intended!

TRANSFORMATION

One thing is for certain—nothing stays the same. For the professional service firm, issues of ownership transition, unexpected events like a challenging economy, planned mergers, or even hostile acquisitions have a decided impact on the brand.

Without other information, clients perceive change as bad, damaging brand image. Focusing part of your brand strategy on transformative events will mitigate that issue and can help strengthen the brand by taking a proactive approach. This is where proactive communication becomes critical.

Mike Reilly comments on the challenge of public relations during a merger or acquisition: *"In mergers and acquisitions, we face the ultimate avoidance exercise. Nobody even wants to name the firms. What the press wants to know is who is acquiring whom, why they are combining, and what does it mean to clients and the industry."*

One of the pitfalls of a mature brand is the risk that it will become stale. While establishing a strong brand can be the strategic backbone of your firm's growth, it is tempting to simply rely on the innovation and acumen that got you there. Success can result in lost momentum, and as a firm becomes larger, it runs the risk of becoming less agile, making it more difficult to respond to changing market conditions.

ON MATURITY

There are plenty of examples of firms who established a strong brand presence during their *"15 minutes of fame,"* only to become a weak brand in their later years. Success is a journey, not a destination. Once you climb the mountain as the exciting up-and-comer, you must push even harder to stay ahead of the next wave of industry innovators all too happy to knock you off the peak.

That doesn't mean abandoning the values and differentiators that have served you well, but you must continually reevaluate their effectiveness in the market and how you apply them to improve the lives of your clients, your clients' clients, and your communities.

GILBANE BUILDING COMPANY: *Family Matters*

The **Gilbane Building Company**, based in Providence, Rhode Island, is one of the largest, privately held, family-owned real estate development and construction firms in the industry. Since 1873, they have leveraged a rich history with extensive knowledge to deliver facility solutions. At the core of their brand is the focus on family and the importance of that connection to their staff and their clients.

Gilbane is composed of two operating companies: Gilbane Building Company and Gilbane Development Company, together providing integrated expertise in finance, property development, planning, and commercial construction. Gilbane has 60 offices and employs 2,500 people.

Chris Watson, national director of marketing services at Gilbane, notes that one of the challenges for a firm with such strong family ties is that as they have expanded nationally, they find that different regions have different expectations. In serving multiple vertical markets that the company started locally, but now practices nationally, communicating a consistent brand message becomes critical.

The Architecture of Image

Gilbane's brand is built on a solid foundation of vision (aspiration) and mission (brand promise). Their vision is that Gilbane will be the premier company serving a full spectrum of client facility needs. Their mission promises "Building more than buildings."

Watson noted that within Gilbane, the idea of brand is extremely important. Because it's the family name, if something tarnishes the brand, it tarnishes the family name. Watson, says, *"You want your brand to be one that people not only recognize, but that they can also trust."*

He commented that one of the amazing things about the Gilbane brand is that if something were to go wrong, the person who gets on the line to make the situation right—the person you talk to—is a Gilbane.

Building a brand-oriented culture at Gilbane is important. Every new employee goes through a three-day on-boarding—with refresher programs every six months—that provides insight into the firm's vision, mission, goals, and values.

Gilbane defines those values as competitiveness, tough mindedness, teamwork, dedication to excellence, loyalty, and discipline. The firm promotes those values externally and internally, and celebrates when their values are exemplified by an employee's actions.

Gilbane's brand stands for integrity, quality, safety, and longevity. They have been working with some clients going back to the 1800s. For new clients, expressing the company's brand is more of a challenge.

Watson says, *"New clients sometimes see us as old and slow, but that is not true. Through our work, we communicate experience and quality. In the end, the vast majority come away with a positive view of the firm's integrity and brand."*

Gilbane monitors its brand rigorously, tracking news in print and online. They conduct regular regional surveys and apply those findings to improve awareness and strengthen brand position.

Gilbane is not shy about embracing social media to extend their brand. They use Facebook, Twitter, YouTube, Flickr, and LinkedIn. Watson notes, *"Everybody is there, we should be, too."* Like many firms, Gilbane looks for ways to make social media valuable and has created a corporate blog written by a core group plus the occasional guest author.

Their social media style is externally facing. They also have internal blogs on their Intranet, where employees can find excellent resources to communicate firm values to clients regarding, lean methodologies, safety, and environmental concerns.

Gilbane has regular company-wide communications, including quarterly web-based meetings led by firm leaders, designed to reinforce the company's message, goals, and vision.

The Architecture of Image

From a marketing perspective, Watson focuses on improving brand presentation and unified message through a library of collateral material, including uniform corporate strategic messaging with customized regional elements, case studies, etc. To differentiate from their competitors, they have developed proprietary analytical and design tools to benefit their clients.

Watson says, *"In a competitive market, what it really comes down to is that while pricing will be an issue, what you say about your services, how you demonstrate the strength of your project executive, and how you present your employees as representations of the brand will be the differentiators."*

Gilbane believes strongly in the power of expert positioning as a way to build brand equity. They utilize public speaking opportunities as an important part of their outreach efforts. They focus on having senior staff present at trade shows and related industry shows, submitting presentations for 40 to 50 engagements a year.

For 140 years, Gilbane's practice has been consistent and authentic—an exemplar of a truly enduring brand.

CHAPTER 6 | Evolution

*What we think, what we know, or what we believe is, in the
end, of little consequence. The only consequence is what we do.*
JOHN RUSKIN

EVERY BRAND GOES THROUGH AN EVOLUTIONARY PROCESS from initial

development to maturity. Adaptation is one of the hallmarks of a

strong brand. With headlines spanning recessions, financial

default, tornados and tsunamis, and alien invasions, there is no

dearth of exclamatory issues to distract you from your vision of

building a strong brand.

With leadership transitions, mergers or acquisitions, or technical

challenges, making scenario planning a key part of your brand

strategy can ensure a thoughtful approach to unexpected

change.

As part of your branding program, ask yourself "what if?"

Developing a scenario-based planning approach can help you

adjust your practice, realign with new market conditions and

demands, and maintain brand position by being flexible,

creative, and cognizant.

Scenario planning is an important part of the strategic planning process. It should also be an important part of your branding strategy. Documenting alternative scenarios that could have a negative impact on the brand can generate a plan of action should something unexpected happen.

With roof and bridge collapses, unexpected flooding, structural failures, or technology system outages, the technical designer is always at the forefront of media attention, often much to the detriment of the brand.

Rapid response by your communication team and rapid reaction by your technical team can go a long way to mitigate negative press. However, without the effort of pre-event scenario planning, it is much more difficult to react quickly and have the appropriate message that will support your commitment and reinforce your brand value.

TRANSITION

Ownership transition can have a major impact on the perception of the brand. It pays to start this process early so that the market is aware of the evolution in leadership and the firm demonstrates consistency in its service delivery. In some ways, it's easier to hire an outsider to take over the firm than it is to elevate an insider to a leadership position.

Mike Reilly comments, *"When a key person is leaving, you have to answer the question 'what does that mean?' The perception by most clients is that there is a diminishing of capability."*

Instead of refuting the misconception, counter with the information about the remaining experts' visibility in the market and how they are demonstrating value. Instead of responding to a loss of expertise, focus on the up-and-coming employees for whom that departure opened the opportunity for them to shine. This injects a note of energy and optimism, externally and internally.

Internally, transition to new leadership is potentially difficult for your staff. Issues of trust and confidence placed in the founding principal will need to be rebuilt with both clients and staff. In every communication of a potential change, leadership must be quick to acknowledge the success of the previous owners and the opportunity to build on that success.

ACQUISITION

Mergers and acquisitions are important aspects of growth for corporate management, finance, and marketing. Strategies that allow a company to grow rapidly without having to build another business unit can reap great rewards. Instead, by buying, selling, or combining different companies, you can maximize market share and stakeholder value.

Mergers or acquisitions often make good business sense and, when done well, can result in a stronger brand with the organization better positioned to succeed in the marketplace. When done poorly, a merger can result in loss of brand value as measured by loss of market share, loss of key staff, and ultimately, financial difficulties.

Lippincott's Wilke notes, *"What we always ask about any merger or acquisition is, 'Is this about being better together or creating something totally new and different?' If it's about, 'We're better together and we can grow better,' that says something about how the identity should come together. If the merger is more revolutionary—i.e., Company A and Company B are coming together to create something completely new and different in the marketplace—that, in turn, might suggest you send a more transformational brand message."*

Wilke continues, *"The name change and the identity strategy really should reflect what the particular intent of the merger is about. In terms of the transition period to a new name, many larger, established firms already have their name splashed around the world—on signs, buildings, vehicles, and sometimes airplanes. We encourage these companies to figure out the right decision and make the change only once—go from what you are now to what the new name is going to be... immediately."*

Most experts agree that the transition time for a name change should be a year or less before the acquired firm becomes an integral part of the parent. Anything longer than that can lead to brand confusion.

SMPS' Worth, notes, *"If the transition focuses on the core competencies and core processes of both firms, it can be a natural progression. Having independent fiefdoms doesn't work for either the buyer or the seller."*

Again, it requires a significant brand-oriented effort to position the new entity as stronger in the eyes of your clients and potential clients. Regardless of the outcome, recent financial industry surveys suggest that building industry mergers and acquisitions are on the rise and the trend is expected to continue.

PSI's Boogher says, *"We have acquired more than 90 firms in 30 years, though that has become less important than organic growth in the last 5 years. We have a fast integration process averaging 3 to 9 months from old name to PSI. We do not waste a lot of time."*

The recent economy has led to a number of significant mergers and acquisitions as larger firms buy small to mid-size firms that are struggling, often through economic or ownership transition challenges, allowing the larger firm to add new services and expand into new geographies.

Wilke adds, *"For professional services firms, it's important to take a very careful look at organic growth versus acquisition growth. If you're a professional services firm, your people are your product. When you acquire people from other cultures, if you don't incorporate them into your culture, it's like finding a worm in the Coca-Cola can. That kind of damage to your brand can be irreparable and destroy the equity of the professional services brand. Our recommendation is for companies to have a fully developed 'employee brand activation' program that is highly sensitized to the dynamics of the merger/acquisition and proactively addresses internal cultural needs."*

When a merger succeeds, it creates a brand advantage; when it fails, it is often because proper attention was not paid to integrating culture and values first. Only time will tell if a merger will strengthen a brand.

ON EVOLUTION

All firm's go through an evolutionary brand process. Nothing is static. Hopefully, expertise, experience, and the quality of your projects improve over time. Your sphere of influence and client awareness will grow, if you are leveraging and communicating your brand promise. Understanding the elements of this natural evolution can help you anticipate opportunities to build your brand.

The Architecture of Image

HGA: *A Culture of Collaboration*

The national architectural and engineering practice, Hammel, Green and Abrahamson, now known as **HGA,** is a good example of a natural evolution of brand name from the original partners' surnames to their current acronym. Throughout their history, they have pursued new design directions through multidisciplinary, knowledge-based design investigation to deliver the greatest value to their clients.

HGA serves their clients from seven offices in the Midwest and West and East Coasts. They focus on several vertical markets including arts community education, healthcare, energy infrastructure, and corporate/public office space.

By understanding their cultural and business needs, HGA helps their clients realize their organization's vision and potential through responsive, innovative, and sustainable design. A key element to their brand as innovators is becoming a strategic partner with their clients, providing primary research into new trends, applications, and approaches to meet their building needs.

The Architecture of Image

HGA publishes white-paper-style monographs on topics of interest to their clients, featuring information they have gathered through their projects.

According to Julie Luers, FSMPS, vice president and director of marketing, *"HGA's brand has three organizing principles. First, understand the voice of the customer. Our services are designed to engage all the stakeholders. The second is process improvement. We seek to find how workflow can be organized to improve client productivity. The third is maximizing value. We bring internal research to the client, aligning expertise with the value that they bring, especially in areas of sustainability and net-zero-plus energy efficiency."*

These are key messages they share with their employees, illustrating what and how they approach and do their work with supporting case studies.

HGA's mission, vision, and values are summarized in a tagline: 'Strength of our ideas; Quality of our solutions.' HGA summarizes its branding message in book form as a reference for all employees. They understand that key messages need to resonate with everyone. The book provides talking points to align the brand message for each of their offices, guiding consistent messaging for all marketing and communication.

HGA's media outreach targets both existing and potential clients. They tailor the message for different markets and geographies based on their tenure in that market, their local/regional competitors, and other factors. In addition, HGA has internal and external blogs, some with individuals under their own bylines, and some that focus on market sectors.

Luers sees the HGA brand reflected in their graphics as providing a unifying standard for print and internet applications. *"At the end of the day, HGA's brand can be defined as thought leadership, collaborators, and design-driven—qualities that clients really want."*

HGA builds brand awareness through education. Their staff speaks at client conferences, authors white papers, and posts on the web. HGA measures brand equity. They track web hits, press pickups, and increases in acquiring targeted clients. They use client surveys and follow-up with what they learn and share perceptions that can inform new projects and better define their value.

HGA exemplifies a strong brand strategy that is embedded in the firm's culture.

The Architecture of Image

PART III
COMMUNICATION | Your Brand *Becomes*

The medium is the message.
MARSHALL MCLUHAN

FOR MARKETING PROFESSIONALS, communication is the practice within the practice of the firm. You are charged with telling your story—in words, images, and impressions—that resonate with your clients. You develop the expression of your message based on the stories behind the solutions your firm provides. You leverage all the appropriate mediums to convey that message.

You create the unique value proposition that states your differentiators. You set the schedule and frequency to ensure the persistence of your message. You measure the results, establishing and documenting return-on-investment expectations. And, you set the stage for an enduring, evolving, brand.

DISTINCTION

Learning to convey and communicate the nature and value of your service is important. The key is to not just differentiate, but to be distinct—in the level of expertise of you and your staff, in the delivery of the service, and in the experience the client has working with your firm.

One of the major challenges facing the professional service business is internal communication. Sharing information from the various functional and market-facing departments that make up the enterprise is critical for any individual to feel connected, involved, and engaged.

Webster's Musil, says, *"Internal communication can use a variety of tools. Make your environment reflect the brand using the interior of the building, environmental signage, and newsletters. They need to be brand intensive, not just in graphics, but in message."*

Many firms acknowledge that having every employee be able to state the brand promise of benefits and values is a challenge, even at the leadership level. However, your goal should be to improve that ability, so that everyone across the firm is able to define your differentiator or 'so what' statement.

PSI's Boogher, adds, *"Our biggest challenge is taking our tagline and making it a reality—to grow the image of the firm as 'one company, one call' to all of our clients. I see this as the low-hanging fruit opportunity to break down the silos within our company and to get our clients to understand how we can provide other services and support their needs in different geographies. That's our branding goal."*

Regardless of role, everyone wants to feel they are contributing. It becomes the mandate for leadership to find ways to tell the stories of the best practices and celebrate the successes of the firm. Developing a venue for sharing information that provides easy input by the leadership, the practice leaders, and especially the staff is critical to disseminating the positive stories that help build and maintain moral and extend the firm's brand to individuals.

THE RIGHT VOICE

Certain issues need to be vetted first, before distributing to the entire company. Recent trends in open social media challenge the corporate gate-keepers' (e.g., IT or marketing communications) ability to control the content or the message. The ability for anyone to post their opinion, good or bad, about the practice, the work, or the staff, must be addressed by CIOs without appearing to limit free speech. Simple editorial review controls are usually the answer.

HGA's Luers notes, *"One important aspect of our brand program is tracking. We track Google alerts and upload to social media sites like Architizer, Facebook, Pinterest, and YouTube. As a result of seeing some of our videos, clients have come forward with information that generated project leads."*

Further, the mandates of fiscal responsibility for the privately-held or publically-traded company to carefully monitor content leads the former toward control and secrecy, while the laws governing the latter require open, if not always honest, exposure of pertinent financial information. However, where possible and prudent, an open dialogue on the fiscal soundness and prognosis for the firm removes questions and fear from those responsible for the *doing* of the work.

One of best opportunities for building a collaborative culture, especially across firms with multiple offices, is to create a regular, meaningful, pertinent, communication platform.

When I served as CMO for Field Devereaux in Los Angeles (now Harley Ellis Devereaux) we produced a regular e-newsletter that focused on:

- **People**—the news about professional accomplishments
- **Clients**—the highlights of work for those served
- **Work**—the best practices and innovations of the practice
- **Success**—exemplary awards and industry recognition

That series became the organizing concept for much of the firm's promotional messaging, including their website. This is a great example of a format that can be used either internally or externally to convey value and enhance your brand image.

Whether print or digital, an internal communiqué can illuminate and share the best of your brand's accomplishments. In this way, everyone in the firm can stand up and proudly say, *"This is a great company to work for!"* This is the definition of brand strength at its best.

The added benefit of collecting these stories is that they make great fodder for postings on Facebook, Twitter, LinkedIn, and other relevant social media outlets.

BENEFICIAL VALUE

"It's all about me" is easy. Professionals love to boast. It's a natural outgrowth of their achievements—technically, financially, or famously. The problem with that focus is that clients don't care, find it annoying, or worse, they see it as egocentric. And that egocentricity is the root of most service engagement challenges.

So why not start fresh? Reframe your position as *beneficial value delivered.* Ask more questions than you answer. Avoid subjective. Embrace objective. Be brutally honest—not to the detriment of a business or personal relationship, but to express opportunity in the form of solutions or directions that address the client's needs. Your needs will get met in the process. Honestly.

Professional service firms provide value by applying expert knowledge in practice areas that are not typically in the core competency of the hiring client's organization. That is the driving factor for the engagement—providing advice and counsel that addresses an unknown or technical challenge that is having a negative impact on the client's goals.

Accountants, architects, design consultants, engineers, financiers, management consultants, organizational development, and technology advisors each add value to a client's need to analyze and develop solutions to facilities, economic, personnel, or communication issues facing their enterprise.

Each of these professions comes with a vocabulary unique to their practice. The best translate their expertise into terminology and supporting explanatory communication that illuminates the issue at hand in language easily understood and applied. They become trusted advisors and enjoy long-term relationships that broaden and deepen over time.

However, much too often, the worst hide behind generalization, complexity, obfuscation, and acronym-laden reportage and presentations that mask or substitute good advice with babel and garble. *'Garbage in, garbage out'* was once the information technologist answer to everything, rather than actually addressing the why of the *'in'* or the definition of *'garbage.'*

You don't have to look very far to find some great—often sad, but very humorous—examples of business-speak, archi-speak, techno-speak, or some really bizarre acronyms used to illustrate the *"synergistic and contextual paradigm-shifting concepts"* that supposedly demonstrate their mastery of the problem (or worse, the solution).[11]

When the results are tallied, the advisors who provide clear, concise data, analysis, and pragmatic (both strategic and tactical) recommendations will build business and brand value.

ON COMMUNICATION

The challenge faced by most professional service firms is that their communication is inward- rather than outward-facing. Communication is the key to business success. It is the foundation of relationships—internal and external—and the best method for building brand awareness. Communication sets expectations, builds trust, and celebrates results.

Those that can communicate their ability to provide solutions will increase their repeat and referral business. Others—who continue to wait for the phone to ring and see clients as only a hazard of the profession—will burn and churn through their customers.

For a stronger brand, be the former, avoid the latter.

---

[11] For an excellent illustration of this issue, I recommend you read Brian Fugere's excellent book, *Why Business People Speak Like Idiots: A Bullfighter's Guide, Free Press, 2005.*

CHAPTER 7 | **Expression**

The computer can't tell you the emotional story. It can give you a design, but what are missing are the eyebrows.
FRANK ZAPPA

ALTHOUGH YOUR LOGO IS NOT YOUR BRAND—your brand is the professional service you deliver, and your client's perception of that service—your graphic design standards are an important element of your brand strategy.

When you look at your graphic standards, are they impactful? Consistent? Persistent? Distinctive? Do you have a memorable logo? Do you use a meaningful tagline to help define what you do and what your brand promises?

And while graphics alone are not the brand in the strictest definition—and too often substituted in the minds of those with a true lack of brand understanding—the visual expressions you use every day must support your message and be closely aligned with your brand identity.

DESIGN

Your logo—and all graphically-related collateral that you produce in or digitally for the Internet—is a reflection of your brand. Developing guidelines that explain the standard elements of your brand's graphics is an important tool. Standards allow you to present your firm consistently and authentically— internally and to your clients, your clients' clients, and your communities.

Many of the best brands in architecture and other visual arts are known for their sense of visual design. Those notable firms in more pragmatic but no less creative or innovative service lines like engineering and construction often take graphical cues from their design cohorts.

Invest the time in creating a strong graphics system that transcends all elements of your marketing and communication program and supports your brand's identity.

IN A FEW WORDS

A note on taglines: they can be very effective when done well— three to five words, informative and inspirational, shorthand for what you do, and implying a result. This is especially important when your firm's name does not implicitly convey what you do.

A tagline can clarify your mission and communicate your brand promise.

Good examples include:

- *"We Do Work That Matters, Every Day"* (Burns & McDonnell, architects and engineers)
- *"One Company, Many Solutions"* (HDR, architects and engineers)
- *"Building What's Next"* (Mortensen Construction)
- *"Helping Project Teams Communicate!"* (Communication Resources Northwest, consulting)
- *"We Shape a Better World"* (Arup, multi-disciplinary engineers)

What can you say in three to five words that defines your brand promise?

Today, there are other options using technology and social media to convey our brand that don't rely as much on a tagline. Well-known firms like Gensler, Turner, and Thornton Tomasetti, among many respected brands in the building industry, have forgone taglines in favor of more direct descriptors of the services.

So if you do choose to create a tagline, make it distinctive and memorable.

ALPHABET SOUP

One of the common branding mistakes occurs with the naming of the firm. No matter what combination of names, words, or adjectives, the tendency internally—often only for expediency's sake—is to shorten the name to an acronym.

Be warned about using acronyms as your firm's name. Because so many professional service firms' designation are made up of the names of one, two, three or more *"founding"* principals — unfortunately, too often no longer with us—you may automatically convert those names to an acronym. But, unless you are the AT&T or IBM of your sector, an acronym is often a difficult way to establish your brand.

While some of the firm's profiled here, including BNIM, HGA, PSI and WET, all derived their current acronymic name from an original list of firm founders (BNIM and HGA) or a more descriptive wordmark (PSI and WET), all have become better known in their markets by their alphabetic name.

That's the point. Acronyms are fine when they come from the client and the community, and are much less effective when they are the firm's foundational name.

Another challenge comes when there are many firms with similar acronyms. You only need to look at all the three-letter architectural firms that begin with an *"H"* (e.g., HOK, HKS, HGA, HGM, etc.) How many potential clients would recognize the derivation from the firm's original name? Or be able to differentiate one from another?

My recommendation: Until your clients, your clients' clients, and your communities are consistently referring to your firm's name as an acronym, don't use it yourself. A good, clear, and concise tagline is a better solution.

WHAT'S IN A NAME?

A wordmark created from a single strong name can be an excellent substitution for a logo. Firm's like construction managers, Turner, architects and interior designers, Gensler, and mechanical/electrical engineers, Arup, all have excellent brand recognition for their founder's last name. General construction firms with single names like Clark, Skanska, and Hill are all recognized as strong leaders and strong brands.

Others like architects and engineers, Leo A Daly, and structural engineers, Walter P Moore, use the founder's whole name (note the missing periods after the middle initial) as a wordmark representation of the firm's familial history, integrity, and consistency.

Much better than a typical company sobriquet like "John R. Smith and Associates" (what do they do?), a single word or name, usually tied with an explanatory tagline, can be leveraged to support your brand identity.

Developing a unique wordmark that avoids the partner's name or list of names is a challenge. Firms with strong and distinctive partner names, like architects, Hnedak Bobo Group or engineers, Buro Happold, are memorable in their own right.

Gensler, long shortened from its original M. Arthur Gensler & Partners, has become one of the most highly recognized and respected brand names in architecture. They are known as much for their position as experts in research and quality design as for their size and scale as one of the largest design practices in the world—clearly an example of a strong and enduring brand.

METAPHOR AND MEANING

Another approach to naming is the use of metaphor. Firms like water feature designers, WET, and architects, RATIO, have wordmarks that speak metaphorically to what they do, where Geotechnologies wordmark is a definitive statement of expertise.

WET's singular focus on water feature design makes their name a perfect choice to communicate their brand. Similarly, RATIO is a natural metaphor for the work of an architect. Geotechnologies leaves no question in the mind of the client as to their expertise in the environmental analysis of geotechnical and geologic issues.

Archimania, a Memphis-based design firm, chose a wordmark that clearly conveys their passion for design. Architect One, a Topeka-based design firm's name sends a clear message about their preeminent vision. Structural Focus, Southern California-based structural engineers, conveys an equally clear description of their expertise.

Architectural firms like the SLAM Collaborative and BSA Lifestructures combine their acronymic heritage with a descriptive wordmark to illustrate their brand promise. Entertainment facilities designers, Populous, drew their name from a mission of creating environments that draw people and communities together for unforgettable experiences.

One of my personal favorite firm names is IDEO, the product and environments designers, known for their 'deep-dive' approach to creative ideas and design.

MulvannyG2's Thompson agrees, *"We respect those firms that focus on creating experience. IDEO is such a great example of a company whose name reflects how they live their brand. I'm inspired by their multi-disciplinary use of people from all walks of life to brainstorm to improve their clients' projects and products."*

Whether founders' name, wordmark or tagline, using metaphor to convey meaning resonates and remains memorable in the minds of your clients and your community long after John R. Smith & Associates have faded from view.

IMPACT

The visual manifestation of your brand starts with your logotype; the words or icon that represents your practice. It is important to convey internally that the logo has been carefully sized and placed—and in some cases altered—to create a graphic element or object that should be treated as such.

The logo should always be thoughtfully composed on a page along with other graphic elements and text.

Tracy Black, says, *"Symbolically, the logotype says 'this is who you are and what you do as a core business.' Every aspect of your logotype should reflect this."*

Black noted that in choosing a font, a serif font can represent tradition, stability, and responsibility. A sans serif font reflects a more contemporary and timeless brand. In italics, a font may appear more forward-thinking or represent speed or responsiveness. There are so many fonts to choose from, but if you are clear about your brand, narrowing down to the ones that best represent it should be easy.

The choice of color is also important and conveys meaning. You can reflect your passion by using red; your bold, confident attitude about the future by using black; that you are clean, contemporary and timeless by using grey or white; or, your commitment to sustainability by using green or blue.

Black adds, *"When choosing colors, think about how they will translate into a black and white representation, which may be required for some logo applications. Also keep in mind that multiple colors or custom colors can be more costly to print."*

She noted that symbols can also be used in combination with type to express your brand. For example, a square can reflect stability, or be placed next to a wordmark to show that you *"think outside the box."* Circles are often used to express a comprehensive approach. You may use other icons or symbols in your business that are meaningful and can be incorporated into a logo that represents your brand.

GUIDELINES

Enforcing brand graphic standards is important. Graphic standards should include guidelines for logo size, logo placement and spacing, logo color applications, and when and when not to mix a graphic elements with text. Your brand standards should be reviewed annually to ensure they reflect current market conditions and the most relevant issues facing your clients, your clients' clients, and your communities.

Black adds, *"Create a how-to guide that explains the standard elements of your brand graphics and the tools you have in place to consistently present yourselves with authenticity, both internally and externally."*

Black recommends that your brand guidelines include, but not be limited to:

- Brand guidelines and standards
- Logo usage
- Typography and fonts
- Photography style and usage

- Graphic strategies (layout, color, typography, etc.)
- Content and language style and standards
- Collateral (brochures, project data sheets, resumes, etc.)
- Proposal templates
- Word processing/spreadsheets/PowerPoint documents (for correspondence including letters/memos, transmittals, invoices, forms, etc.)
- Office and jobsite signage
- Swag (giveaways, leave behinds, logo wear, etc.)
- Websites (internet, intranet, extranet)

THE MEDIUM

While distinctive graphics and enforced graphic brand standards are important in the overall brand strategy, unique content and client-facing positioning sets you apart. The vehicles for distinctive communication can include:

- Advertising
- Annual reports
- Books/monographs
- Direct mail
- Feature writing
- Holiday cards/programs

- Market-focused magazines

- Multimedia and 3d design

- External newsletters

- Internal newsletters

- Social media

- Special events, trade shows, and sponsorships

- Specific project- and market-targeted pieces

- Recruiting programs

- Community involvement

Your challenge is to have graphics and content that complement each other. Use simple graphics with a clear message and visuals that can stand alone. Analyze each element of your communication program for its ability to successfully support your brand. Be sure to also look at all elements of your internal and external communication collectively, to evaluate how they work together to create a consistent and comprehensive view of your brand.

EFFECTIVE COLLATERAL

While not the be all to end all to a brand program, it is important to have marketing collateral that reflects and aligns with your company's brand identity as part of your image strategy.

In an era of *design as a differentiator*, it is equally important that the material reflects a design aesthetic that is also aligned with your identity/image (e.g., conservative, high tech, hip, or environmental, etc.). Your message should be simple and straightforward (*"Don't make me think"*), and graphics and production value should reflect an appropriate level of quality.

If you need a non-personal introduction, have someone they know, who also knows you, introduce you. If you can't do that, your network isn't deep enough (yet). If you need a leave behind, have a business card. If you need a follow-up, send a hand-written note expressing gratitude for the meeting, or a typewritten letter summarizing your understanding of their needs and the next steps you will take to address them—not more about you.

THE CRUTCH

Unfortunately, a good brochure is only a small part of your marketing strategy. At best it is a tactic to send ahead or leave behind to remind the client of who you are and what you do and why they should care.

Not having a brochure is not an excuse to not do business development, though many business developers seem to be afraid to go out the door without one. Having a brochure that reflects the company's brand but not your personal design aesthetic is not an excuse to not go to market, but too many business developers think that the competitor's high-level graphics gives them a competitive edge.

A good business developer only needs a phone, a pen, and a credit card to do as much business as they need to generate for their company. Some would say they just need a phone, but, on occasion, they should pick up the lunch tab. And it helps to have a place to capture data about the prospect or client to input into your client relationship management (CRM) system, assuming you have one.

The collateral crutch is a common problem in professional services firms where technical staff—used to doing the work — is put in the uncomfortable position of having to sell the work.

Inexperienced at relationship development, they fall back on *portfolio presentation* as the only story to tell. That's not always a bad thing, but it won't close the deal. The same issue is often exacerbated by business developers whose skills seem sufficient when times are good (i.e., work is readily available), but whose personality *quirks* become much more evident when times are challenging.

My advice to you, your business developers, and your technical *"doer-sellers"* is to get on the phone, set up a meeting, get out of the office, ask good questions, and follow-up. *Do what you say!* And leave the brochure behind.

To be sure, it is important to spend time with the members of your technical staff that have business development responsibilities, explaining all the collateral options you have. They will be more effective when helping customize a qualifications statement or proposal that is not just pre-printed boilerplate, but actually speaks directly to clients' issues and needs. That type of collaboration builds brand image every time.

ON EXPRESSION

Where a memorable name, a simple, clear logo, graphically engaging collateral, and an interactive website may illustrate and reflect your company's brand, ultimately it will be the quality of your service, the innovative solutions you deliver, and the thought leadership you provide that will cause your brand to have longevity in the marketplace.

RATIO

RATIO Architects: *A Promise of Integrity*

RATIO is an interdisciplinary design practice offering services in architecture, historic preservation, interior design, landscape architecture, urban design and planning, and graphic design. They are based in Indianapolis, with offices in Champaign, Chicago, and Raleigh.

The firm offers a wealth of experience in the higher education, community, K-12, life sciences, workplace, lifestyle and cultural marketplaces.

In 1989, the firm changed its name from HDG Architects to RATIO. Tim Barrick, FSMPS, principal, comments, *"We wanted a name that had nothing to do with the partners' names, but instead reflected the talents of the whole firm. We decided on the name RATIO. Ratio is the root word for rational, 'to reason,' 'logical,' and Latin for 'to consider.' Our logo is the golden section, which embodies what we do as a firm—rational, well-proportioned, excellent design. We believe our name and graphic image say a lot about who we are."*

The firm's tagline of *"Defining spaces, creating places, enhancing community"* evolved from the work they do. To ensure that their brand image is consistent with what they do, RATIO surveys their clients every three years to see how they are recognized. They consistently get positive feedback for their outreach.

RATIO is known by potential clients for quality and a high level of service. Barrick says, *"Good design is seen as real value. Our brand is well established and aligns with what our clients understand."*

The brand challenge remains, as with most firms, in getting all employees to understand and be able to express the brand's value. The firm has embarked on that effort as an internal program to address the changes that have resulted from two mergers.

Barrick noted, *"With each merger, we spend a lot of time on conveying and combining culture, but we haven't spent enough time on the psyche of the whole firm."* He sees the challenge in helping the employees not only know what their name and tagline mean, but also understand more about the bigger vision of the firm.

Barrick, adds, *"Brand is important more today than 10 years ago. When we began our branding program, many of our staff thought it was gimmicky, but over time they became believers. Not all architects understand the value of brand. Because of our branding effort, we're known in each of our regions by the buyers of architectural services."*

Like many firms, RATIO has dabbled with social media. Barrick noted that consistency is an issue, with a need for constant content and focus on the brand message. Today, the partners all contribute to the company's blog. Barrick adds, *"They can write about anything, and they write about everything. We think it personalizes our practice."*

One brand differentiator that RATIO has identified is that clients see them as masterful in the use of technology. Barrick notes, *"While everybody uses BIM, we use it differently. We believe our 'LiveDesign' approach of embedding technology in the client's site is unique."* They track statistics on results that demonstrate time saved and accuracy, and then share these results in terms of bottom-line savings to the client.

Barrick notes, *"One of our brand strategies going forward is positioning market specialists to participate in national and regional programs for specific market sectors. It is one area that is not as vigorous as I would like."*

As a firm that has grown through the merger and acquisition process, Barrick notes the importance of unifying the brands. They typically co-brand the acquired firm (such as 'RATIO/SRA') for a year. He comments, *"They remember the first name, so the eventual shift to just RATIO is easier."*

The brand consolidation effort includes an aggressive public relations and mailing campaign combined with events and receptions for former and potential clients.

The Architecture of Image

Barrick emphasized the importance of charting changing client perceptions. They use a survey process, conducted by an outside consultant, who puts together questions and then surveys employees, clients, and prospective clients.

The questions have changed as the firm has evolved. Barrick says, *"As we have grown, some clients might not be aware, even though we've done the mailings. We survey because we want to be sure we haven't confused our brand."*

For key performance indicators, RATIO tracks project performance based on profitability as an indicator of the projects to pursue. Barrick notes, *"As we measure, we look for the project types where we are successful and those where we are not. We focus our marketing efforts on the former and avoid the latter."*

He also noted that because of their more rigorous decision-making process, their hit rate actually dropped, but ultimately improved as they focused on the project types where they had the most success.

Barrick concludes, *"To maintain our brand strength, we seek certain kinds of work and do not stray too far from what we do best."*

CHAPTER 8 | Resonance

*Just because digital technology makes connecting possible
doesn't mean you're actually reaching people.*
MAUREEN DOWD

WITH BRAND STANDARDS IN PLACE, the real issue becomes
communicating your brand message—the content that defines
your value in terms of benefit and relevance supported by proof.
What medium will you use to convey your message? What
frequency will you use to ensure that your message persists in
the mind of the buyers of your service?

Many firms create a vision and mission statement, a set of
fundamental values, or a tag line to reinforce their core values as
a message to their employees and clients. If they ring true to the
experience of working with you, they add to brand value. If your
aspirations don't ring true they are more likely to simply sit on a
shelf or be framed as a poster on the wall. These only serve as
reminders of what you want to be, but show you are not
committed to actually achieving them. In the end, non-action will
damage your brand.

The Architecture of Image

Regardless of print, electronic, and digital content, your message should pull the potential buyer into your sphere of influence, where their response is *"opt in!"* or *"tell me more!"*

Further, the same consistency should be heard in the personal effort made by your principals, business developers, and technical *"doer-sellers"* as they take your message directly to the field, person-to-person.

While we live in a world inundated with radio, TV, pop-up ads, and Google key-word advertisers, very few have any effective application for the professional service firm.

PSI's Boogher says, *"At one point, we spent a lot of time and money on advertising. I've come to the conclusion that no amount of advertising can replace the importance of how your firm operates, delivers its work, and is perceived in the marketplace. The efforts of your managers and staff, how you interact with clients, the networking that you do, the societies that you belong to, and the leadership roles you take on are far more important to your brand than any amount of money you spend on advertising efforts."*

Better, to meet your long-term goals, know that it will take a transformational change in everything you do. A key will be how your people become actively involved in the right professional societies, associations, community groups, and philanthropic organizations to not just work in—but to contribute to—the communities you serve.

MESSAGE

A public relations program starts with your brand message. Before any PR is done, you have to figure out what is the most valuable thing you can talk about.

Mike Reilly, notes, *"If firms are most inclined to talk only about their projects, which most firms are inclined to do, it's a missed opportunity to go up the ladder to focus more on the value of lessons learned and what matters to the client."*

There's an old saying that it's not as important as where to go with your message as it is what to say. Reilly adds, *"Editors consistently tell us that they get insignificant information that is project based or people based, but not value based."*

The Architecture of Image

What editors look for is a story—not simply a project—or an innovation, or a passion. The key is translating the experience your firm brings to a project, innovation, or passion into a story with controversy or conflict.

Reilly says, *"As an industry, we tend to only talk about those issues that are not conflicted or controversial, like issues of challenge, perseverance, and overcoming obstacles to meet a client's goals. What's newsworthy is a story that captures the reader's imagination and defines the benefit brought to the project."*

Who is your target audience? What is your objective for the piece? How will it be used to support your current marketing efforts? What are the three most important things you want to communicate to your target audience? What do you want the reader to see first? These are all questions that need to be asked before you start a PR program.

What action do you hope the reader will take? How is your firm different from your competition in a way that benefits the client? Is your contact information easy to find? If the piece is commercially printed, consider excluding items that will date the piece too quickly.

With the cacophony of information available today, learn to write for skimmers. Create headings that are informative and draw in/involve the reader. Put all main ideas upfront. Consider turning headings into benefits, relevance, or proofs. Organize sections to be logical and easy to follow. Use short and direct sentences.

Break long paragraphs into bite-size lengths. Use bulleted lists instead of long paragraphs. Highlight your firm's differentiators, not just features. Explain how what you bring to the table has worked in unique and innovative ways for similar clients. Facts tell, but stories sell!

SAY WHAT MATTERS

Have you ever been faced with the irony that everything you thought was true is wrong? Drawn from our experiences—good and bad, informing and humbling, nurturing, and demoralizing—when challenges arise, can you apply that learning to each new opportunity and challenge?

Your brand is based on the quality of your relationships. As you create, build, and enhance your practice, you trust that the expertise and experience you bring to your clients will be seen as valuable. Where you miss the mark is when you believe that your expertise and experience is invaluable.

Realize that each party in a contractual relationship brings a unique and self-aware—if not necessarily self-centered, then certainly self-centric—view. We each have an idea of the impact and what results of our engagement will yield. Ego is the root cause of most client/consultant rifts, especially when you, the consultant, forget the age-old wisdom of *"the client is always right."*

RATIO's Barrick notes *"Make sure your culture understands that you are all marching to the same drummer. As we come out of a stagnant market, you can lose sight of your mission and vision. It is critical to readopt and reinforce the message of those values as you see the market improve. It is important to maintain forward momentum."*

Forgoing ego is a real challenge. It is far too easy to attach expectation to our own pre-defined image of the outcome. This is not to say there is no power in intention. Short- and long-term goals help us visualize and realize our dreams. Getting there remains a step-by-step process of applying our practice to the practice.

Bright Operations' Banning-Wright, adds, *"New clients often have the perception of having known me for years, because I've been visible in the business. Now, the more I can let people know through my dialogue with them, through my website, or my seminars and presentations, the more they will completely understand what I'm about and what Bright Operations is about. Being visible saves them and me time."*

Focusing on mutually agreed upon goals and communicating openly, honestly, and regularly will help you overcome questions of intention, performance, or value.

The best brands are known for value-based solutions, which have usually come as the result of experiences drawn from a mistake, miscalculation, or failure. Those that rise from a misstep to formulate better, more informed counsel will ultimately be seen as the stronger brand.

There is no obligation to our client relationships beyond that. Isn't it ironic? Sincere, genuine, authentic, innovative, and inspirational define the strongest brands in the professional services arena.

THE RIGHT MEDIUM

Press Release? Multimedia Release? Print? Web? E-mail? TV? Radio? LinkedIn, Facebook, Twitter, Flckr, Pinterest, YouTube? Blogs? Conferences? Seminars? Special Events? Which is the most effective in telling your brand story? In an era of information overload, the answer is probably *"all of the above."*

In this era of social media, you may be able to influence your brand somewhat, but constant postings seem a little self-promoting and shallow, if you don't have substance behind what you say.

Webster's Musil adds, *"Our advice on social media is that your brand must be consistent across all client-facing outlets, even where the perceived audiences are different (i.e., Facebook v. LinkedIn or Twitter v. YouTube). If they see different positioning or faces of the brand they can become confused. We advise different solutions dependent on your needs, but we preach consistency."*

On the whole, the building industry is late in its acceptance and use of social media. Most of the industry's appications might be described as embryonic. While many have initiatives that are studying social media including blogs, Twitter, LinkedIn, and

Facebook., there is general agreement that social media is a branding opportunity, but few are using it effectively yet.

The choices you make on how and where to deliver your message are critically important to building your brand image. Rather than delving into a lengthy discussion on trends in social media, which are important, I'll focus on the basics of public relations, or PR.

While social media is important as a vehicle for communication, understanding that "value perceived" in the information you post—by your clients, potential clients, and your communities— is all that is important. In the case of social media, the medium is *not* the message, it is only the medium.

ALL PR IS GOOD PR

The process of public relations is defined as the communication of your understanding of your firm's brand value. It is how you communicate the firm's identity and objectives to the media through stories about people and projects and their related benefits, relevance, and proof.

Implicit in this process are procedures to evaluate the effectiveness of promotional activity and the impact of all media-based promotional efforts, regardless of venue.

The Architecture of Image

The public relations process encompasses business/social etiquette and protocol, trade show event management, and industry/media/civic events. Your PR effort provides an outlet for your expertise and your brand's value. You can use PR to promote your firm's credentials and differentiate your company from your competition.

Public relations is one of the most powerful tools for building recognition of your company's services and elevating the value you provide to a wide audience of potential new customers. Your public relations program manages communication between your organization and its key stakeholders, with a focus on building and maintaining a positive and valuable brand image.

Typically, a public relations program involves:

1. **Evaluating** public exposure, opinions, and attitudes
2. **Developing** policies for communicating with the media and the public
3. **Implementing** communication programs across multiple media channels
4. **Integrating** public communications with marketing programs and brand
5. **Creating** goodwill by managing a two-way communication process

6. **Building** a positive relationship between the public and the organization

Taking the message and leveraging the medium still require a strategy for publicity. What outlets, at what frequency, and at what scale all impact the effectiveness of your brand story.

Press, (whether print or digital), media (whether TV, radio, or the Internet equivalents), and social media (Twitter, LinkedIn, Facebook, et al.) relations remain one of the least leveraged tools in the professional service firm's marketing kit of parts. Like good client relations, good media relations rely on *relationships.* And that's where the challenge lies.

We are finally at the point where there is no just analog approach to public relations. A good example is Twitter. Because of editor preferences for research through social media first, following us using traditional print PR second can make sense.

There has been a great migration by editors who use Twitter as a source or virtual search engine to find out about what is being said about a particular topic. Because of this, any public relations campaign needs to include social media in the overall strategy.

CREATING A CAMPAIGN

First, identify the press, media, or social media outlets that your target clients follow and respect. Those publications can range from local news and business press to regional, national, or international periodicals to the Twitter feed of an industry analyst.

Next, you need to know who—editors and reporters—are covering your firm and competing firms that look like you. What stories of interest seem to get the most ink?

There is a lot of great information not specifically related to architecture or engineering that comes from other service industries that you can adapt for your firm.

Gilbane's Watson agrees, *"Anyone who fails to realize that other industries offer interesting ideas is selling their company short. I'd look at technology companies, especially if you are looking to expand globally."*

What are the issues of business process, design, finance, or litigation headlining the insight reflected in the daily, weekly, and monthly news sources your clients are following?

Finally, develop a regular, routine, and consistent media engine to distribute your *important* news—the news that is targeted and tailored to meet the goals of those publications that your clients read.

One of the most common mistakes most professional service firms make is to use public relations only for self-promotion—highlighting their recent *"win," "new hire," "promotion,"* or *"award."* Some of these will get picked up as a paragraph on a back page, but rarely will they be so newsworthy as to garner more comprehensive coverage.

While potentially newsworthy, a press release about *"contractor selection"* is really only relevant when the project represents a significant dollar value. *"Groundbreaking ceremonies"* with quotes from the political and leadership in attendance might make good political sense, but probably not editorial sense.

Should you continue to create this type of press release? Yes. Even though they are less effective, they are important because they can help you learn to write more effectively, if you solicit feedback as you build editorial relationships.

And, they keep your brand in front of editors and reporters, even though they are not really differentiating. The news only about your firm is usually and ultimately forgettable.

More effective is an investment in building personal relationships with those publishers, editors, and reporters that you respect, rather than relying solely on blanket mail, fax (yes, some still do), or email releases, that ultimately wastes time and energy—yours and theirs.

The important news releases are those stories that relate directly to your target audiences' goals. Those get read and remembered. More importantly are those stories that define value provided in terms of demonstrated benefit. These can be leveraged as reprints and redistributions to past, current, and potential clients, providing third-party validation of the message you want to be read and remembered. In fact, these reprints can become some of the most effective collateral material in your marketing and business development toolkit.

PERSISTENCE

Consider these *best practices* for effective and persistent public relations strategy:

1. Evaluate your target audiences such as customers, prospects, partners, suppliers, etc. and segment them into relevant sub-categories.

2. Talk to representatives from your target audience categories to identify where they go for information related to your organization and industry.

3. Create a high-level list of potential media outlets that correspond to your customer information sources.

4. Look for online editions of your media outlets to identify journalists that would be appropriate to contact. Develop a relationship with these people as they have a large influence over what content will be published.

5. There are three traditional distribution options: newswire, media database, or individual correspondence. Most PR applications automate the delivery process and can provide substantial contacts for your industry.

6. Consider social media as a component of your media distribution strategy. More and more editors are finding story ideas and publishing links for news pushed through blogs, Facebook, LinkedIn, Twitter, Flickr, Pinterest, and other social media sites.

7. Avoid the end of fiscal quarters or year-end, as many large organizations will be flooding the media with their results. Do not lose your message in the clutter. If you are

launching a new service, or opening an office, for example, identify the optimal time to send your message, i.e. two weeks prior to the event in a specific geographic region.

8. Monitor and measure what matters. Review results using the monitoring and measuring services available in the marketplace. Track your media exposure and evaluate based on specific, set goals. Are you getting exposure through your top-targeted media outlets on a regular basis?

The best relationships you can build with your targeted media outlets will not only yield regular publication of your news, but can position you as the media's go-to expert in your market.

Mike Reilly, adds, *"What editors look for is a story, not simply a project, or an innovation, or a passion. The key is translating the experience you bring to a project into a story with controversy or conflict. Every great story has conflict."*

If you are consistently reliable not only for pushing out solid content and story ideas, but also for being responsive to media deadlines and needs, they will begin to pull you into breaking stories for input and commentary, or important opportunities for by-lined pieces. Ultimately, this is the most cost- and brand-effective media exposure you can gain.

The return on investment in public relations is quantifying the results from that activity. When you can point to a project or revenue that came from a public relations effort, you can clearly measure its value.

However, it is often difficult to quantify because of the lag between publication to referral or project. The more immediate ROI comes when there is a response through social media. If there is a conversation, where the audience comments or re-Tweets on what you have said or done, you have brand enhancement.

Regularly demonstrate that you have published, spoken, and won awards—consistently communicate what you do and how you have been recognized for what you do.

PERSONAL PRACTICE

Like public relations, the business development effort is equally important to building brand awareness. Like all marketing efforts, it requires patience and persistence. From the outset, making cold calls is a tiring effort. For every ten calls, you might get one meeting. And it probably takes three to ten calls to even get to the conversation to set the meeting. That's 100 calls.

From the first meeting, it may take two to five additional meetings, spread over several months, to know enough about the client and their needs to:

1. Ensure you have the right skills to address those needs
2. Know the key drivers to make an appropriate proposal that they will find beneficial for its cost
3. Convey your brand's value to them

Assuming they show interest, it may still take several weeks to several months to see the effort lead to a request for qualifications or proposal and to see the proposal become a contract. What most business developers don't understand is the machinations that most organizations go through when any significant amount of time, money, effort, or energy is about to be committed.

While the direct users of your services may see the immediate value, their management—and especially those in finance—may raise new questions regarding need, value, and timing in the context of their organization's broader priorities.

While the business developer can help the user with additional data to help them circumvent and pass through the hurdles, most of the time it falls back to their internal relationships to get the project approved and moving foward. In a challenging economy, the hurdles are more numerous and higher, further impacting the schedule from initial desire to fulfillment.

A good business developer needs to be persistent—to a point. Knowing that point—and respecting the customer—can go further to strengthen the relationship and the brand perception than pushing so hard that the customer seeks another solution.

POINT OF NO RETURN

While persistence is important, it can work against your goals. For example, a business developer from a service firm had demonstrated that his service would do exactly what a client needed. However, the client's internal structures and concern for the coming fiscal year's performance delayed their ability to commit to the service. The client knew this frustrated the business developer to no end. Unfortunately, in his persistence to close the deal, the business developer started to voluntarily cut his cost. And while that discount might help with the client's budget constraints, it did nothing for his bottom line or their expectation for service. This approach can quickly become a vicious circle, where the quality of service will be, by necessity, diminished by the reduction of appropriate fee.

To improve his position, he could have acknowledged the delay and asked for the best future time to continue the conversation. Instead, he called every morning—like clockwork—and got the same response: *"We're working on the approval, and expect to know in the next few weeks. We'll call you."*

In the end, this process only frustrated the client further and brought them to the point of reevaluating whether his was the right service solution for their initiative after all.

Tracy Black notes, *"The other issue regarding cutting fee is that it leaves the client wondering why the initial fees were so high that they could be so easily cut. It brings to question the business developer's—and by inference, the firm's—integrity."*

ON RESONANCE

To improve brand position, first identify what is truly different about your firm, process, clients, and employees. What is significant and notable? What do clients say about you? If you don't know, you have to ask.

Every company has a competitive advantage that comes from identifying those differentiators and translating them into marketing and PR communication. If you do research, even just post-occupancy, it can be a valuable part of the brand message.

By demonstrating the inclination to research and apply lessons learned, you demonstrate that collaboration is part of the brand.

Resonance defines the quality of the communication and expression of your brand within your practice. If there is a disconnect between what you say you are and how you (and your staff) practice, the difference will destroy any credibility in your brand.

Use the media to build awareness. However, it will be personal relationships that cause that awareness to resonate with the client, and are critical to your long-term success and communicating brand value.

The Architecture of Image

WET: *Remarkable*

WET, long the acronymic shorthand for Water Entertainment
Technologies is a water feature design firm based in Los Angeles,
with branch offices in Dubai and Beijing and a staff of 125. WET is
probably best known for its design of the nine-acre Fountains of
Bellagio in Las Vegas, but the company has also designed more than
two hundred fountains and architectural water features all over the
world.

WET takes project pursuit seriously. Teresa Powell-Caldwell, vice
president, says, *"Our criterion for getting involved is that the result
will be something that is memorable and remarkable. Our goal is
that you can't walk past one of our features without stopping."*

As a technology-oriented company, WET struggles with the idea of
a fixed mission statement. Powell-Caldwell says, *"We evolve so fast
that we can never seem to find a mission that sticks. I guess we
could say, 'We create projects that bring pleasure to people, draw
people to a place, and they stay.'"*

The Architecture of Image

For a design firm like WET, the idea of brand is very important. Powell-Caldwell notes, *"For us, brand is huge, beyond huge. We think of ourselves in a league of our own. As the firm that really pioneered show fountains, we have always been at the cutting edge of that industry. Our brand is everything. We will never license our name, and we don't design or manufacture for others."*

WET's brand is seen by owners, architects, and landscape architects as the power to differentiate. They are known for creative innovation that makes a difference in the place-making experience.

Another aspect of WET's brand program is a focus on both flawless quality and innovation. Powell-Caldwell notes, *"We want people to say, 'Whenever we want something highly innovative or creative, we think of WET.' We want that to extend to all we do, and not be just about fountains."*

WET tracks client perceptions throughout the design, manufacturing, and installation process. They conduct a client survey at substantial completion of each project, and check back after the project has been operational for some time.

To ensure that they gather client feedback on process and results, the business development staff stays involved throughout the whole project. Powell-Caldwell notes, *"By acting in a client service role, they ensure the experience is what we promise."*

She notes that WET employees are evangelists for the firm and new work often comes from their dialogue with others. She says, *"When we hire, we look for passion."* Each employee goes through a two-week emersion program that includes orientation and project visits.

To maintain consistency in internal and external messaging, their newsletter features staff stories on how they came to WET. She says, *"100-percent have a story, ranging from 'I proposed to my wife in front of the Bellagio fountain' to 'when I first came to the US, I saw Epcot...'"*

One of WET's differentiators is being first to design a unique feature. Powell-Caldwell notes, *"It is not that hard to differentiate when you talk facts, but the stories we tell go even further and are drawn from the passion that comes from our employees and our clients for the experience of our work."*

WET's business development efforts focus on story. They approach each client with the goal of creating a relationship that will result in a great story. And, they share those stories at client conferences with topics that range from the latest fountain design to water scientists speaking on water quality.

Powell-Caldwell comments on the brand as an element of their pursuit strategy, saying, *"We spend more time determining if clients are a good fit, so our hit rate is nearly 100 percent. While some of the analysis is subjective, much is based on their ability to fund, execute, and maintain the project. For us, nothing is worse for the brand than a water feature that is no longer in use."*

As an illustration of their creative look at brand and marketing programs, WET is working with their clients to develop a phone/tablet app that will allow visitors to a fountain site to request certain music to be played with their fountain experience.

One of WET's brand objectives is to overcome the perception that they are too expensive. Powell-Caldwell notes, *"We design features all across the cost spectrum, but the big ones are the most noted, so people wrongly assume that is all we do. The process is difficult, because most of our projects have an 'it's never been done before' quality. In a competitive market, we have to change client perceptions by continually showing innovation and place-making value."*

CHAPTER 9 | **Results**

At the beginning of the day, it's all about possibilities.
At the end of the day, it's all about results.
BOB PROSEN

HOW DO YOU KNOW you are getting the brand equity results you want out of your brand-building program? Simply, measure what matters.

Brand equity for the professional service firm is as challenging to measure as return on investment (ROI) is for marketing. For marketers, it is often a sense or a feeling—the *"buzz"* as business gurus Tom Peters or Seth Godin might say. But for management—if brand and marketing efforts are to be credible—equity also needs to be factual.

To start, define a set of goals that describe the results you want. Then create measurable actions that reflect your goals. By defining a set of metrics that regularly monitor and measure your success, you will be able to demonstrate true return on investment for your marketing dollars and its impact on your brand equity.

The Architecture of Image

What do those marketing metrics typically look like? Many use a set of industry benchmarks, such as hit rates, new contract volume, revenue, marketing expenses, and the like. Then track the numbers—and their upward or downward trends—on a regular basis and celebrate or adjust accordingly.

Others track more general—but usually more difficult to actually quantify—measures, including:

- **Differentiation:** The defining characteristics of the brand and its distinctiveness relative to competitors.

- **Relevance:** The appropriateness and connection of the brand to a given consumer.

- **Esteem:** Consumers' respect for and attraction to the brand.

- **Knowledge:** Consumers' awareness of the brand and understanding of what it represents.

While these impressions may be gathered and summarized from survey results, they are harder to put in terms of real dollars. Other more financial measures, like market share, have greater relevance, but are equally difficult to ascertain when your share of a market is very small.

In the business-to-consumer space, if a company or product holds more than 15 percent of an established market, they are considered a market leader. However, for most professional service firms, except the very largest, their percentage of the total market is infinitesimal to the point of irrelevance.

As an example, there are approximately 17,500 architectural practices in the United States today, but the top firms each represent much less than five percent of the total annual billings for this area of practice. The vast majority represent significantly smaller shares of the market.

With numbers like that for most firms, brand recognition for value delivered is far more important than a measure of market share. Incremental increases in key performance areas like annual revenue, opportunity pipeline growth, and success statistics can provide the professional service with a more immediate understanding of the firm's brand equity position.

RELEVANT INSIGHT

While important in informing your brand equity analysis, do these broader metrics really tell us what you need to know? If you are failing in one area, do they give clues as to what you can do to improve? Do they help support, and even drive, the type of behavior that can create the improvements needed? In most cases, you may say that they don't—but should.

PSI's Boogher comments on the importance of financial analysis: *"We can slice and dice a disciplined financial approach to our practice. We can track revenues increasing or decreasing, repeat clients, and percent market-share changes. Are we gaining or losing market share, fees, and sales?"*

RESULTS v. DRIVERS

To effectively measure brand equity, consider the difference between results and drivers. Making sure that your metrics address both provides opportunity to create a more strategic view.[12]

Tracy Black says, *"While some of your metrics may be the typical results-oriented industry benchmarks, it is even more important that you develop metrics that encourage and monitor behaviors that you know will support and drive up your results and help you ultimately reach your goals."*

---

[12] Black, Tracy, *What You Measure Matters*, Zweig-White Marketing Now, September 2010, p. 4

She added that finding your drivers will take some investigation. For example, if you aren't achieving your proposal hit rate goals—and not many of us are in this economy—then you really need to figure out what would drive you to be more successful.

Black noted that many firms slip too easily into a shotgun approach to project pursuits to increase opportunity backlog. She says, *"Chasing any project is a typical management reaction to achieve a firm-wide, results-oriented industry benchmark, but ultimately does not achieve desired results of conversion of opportunity to a contract."*

However, looking back to when your hit rates were better, or knowing intuitively what behaviors need to be improved, you may realize that focusing more resources on fewer project pursuits is a better plan.

So why not develop metrics that encourage and reward those driving behaviors? You could set a goal for a maximum number of proposals for the year and a minimum amount to spend on each one.

Black adds, *"Your staff might think differently if they knew that they had to achieve their backlog goals with only a few proposals, but were given the resources to do each one well enough to win.*

You may start to see some very strategic behavior, and as a result, your hit rates would likely increase."

ONE SIZE DOES NOT FIT ALL

When it comes to strategic metrics, one size does not fit all. If you think about all the variables at play—firm size, corporate culture and vision, services offered, geographic location, and reach—how could one formula determine what works for every firm?

Black says, *"You need to look for what makes your firm perform at its highest levels and build your metrics around supporting those behaviors. You will see the importance of aligning your marketing metrics with other firm-wide metrics. If any of your metrics conflict with one another, you will have a tough time driving the strategic cultural changes needed to make improvements."*

For example, if one of your firm's strategic initiatives is to function seamlessly across geographic locations, then use caution when monitoring performance by geographic location.

Black notes that if leaders of an office are paid bonuses based on their office's hit rate performance, then this structure could discourage working with other offices in ways that would benefit the winning percentages of the entire firm and encourage cross-office cooperation. If they are only compensated on local profitability it could discourage using resources from other locations.

However, if they are measured on percentage contribution to the whole, including a percentage for joint-office efforts—a rising tide raises all boats, as the old saying goes—it can instinctively drive more collaborative behaviors.

Black adds, *"You also can't ignore the reality of external factors— like increased competition or reduced opportunities—so you have to consider current market conditions when developing your metrics. And you will need to adjust them from time to time, to align them with changing firm strategies and keep them reasonable to achieve in the current business environment."*

QUALITY v. QUANTITY

Another thing to consider is developing metrics that drive the quality of your brand, and the resulting marketing performance. For example, if your goal is to expand your brand, then find metrics that measure the quality of your branding activities. You might have a metric for winning awards, but are they the award programs that are most respected by your clients?

Black notes, *"You may have a metric for media clippings, but are you publishing authored articles in client-facing trade publications or just getting a few lines of ink for a new hire in the local business journal? For your social media, don't just look at the number of followers on Twitter, Facebook, or LinkedIn, but monitor your ranking of influence in your industry."*

Analyze your metrics where they strategically relate and help identify behaviors of success. For example, if you have a Go/No-Go pursuit analysis system, use it to see how it compares to your hit rates. Is there a scoring threshold that predicts a better outcome? Are certain criteria a better predictor of success?

A METRICS SYSTEM

To understand strategic metrics for your firm, first look at your strategic plan, mission, vision, and values. These are the results that your metrics must ultimately support and validate.

Then look for patterns of past success and dig deep to figure out what behaviors drive those successes. Finally, examine your existing metrics and industry benchmarks, and build the system that you believe will truly create the results you want.

Black concludes, *"Reward successes accordingly and adjust annually. Your management will appreciate your ability to measure brand results. A clear, concise, and organized brand campaign is one that integrates across all aspects of your practice."*

Your brand development effort will highlight your differentiators and set you apart from your competition. And, finally, you can quantify brand equity through the additive financial benefit of having a strong brand.

BUSINESS BAROMETERS

Looking backward through a rear view mirror is always a difficult way to drive. When it comes to analyzing financial results and finding trends that can help predict the future, it is critical that they are timely. If your accounting systems do not provide current, real-time data, it can be very difficult to react quickly or appropriately.

However, monitoring past results can—like the barometer that predicts change in the weather—provide financial insight showing where the business is trending. In an economy that is at best uncertain and often uncooperative, barometers can foretell that changes are coming and give you the time to adjust your marketing strategies.

As a result, you can put greater effort into managing the business development process to ensure that best practices are being applied and that the visible pipeline is increasing in potential value.

There are several factors that contribute to a barometric dashboard that can help you see trends and provide the reference points used to take corrective action. Tracking month-over-month results of new business (contracts), net fees (billings less consultants), work on hand (backlog), quantity of submittals (proposals), submittal value (weighted potential fee), marketing expense (all costs tied to a particular market or pursuit), and wins (the raw number of new projects) can yield valuable information that can be displayed graphically.

One tool I learned from working with Peter Devereaux, now president and CMO for architects and engineers, Harley Ellis Devereaux, was a long-term-average look at key performance indicators.

Charting using a 12-month trailing average model (the average of the current month and previous 11 months), creates a simple barometric display that—blending real-time and historic data—provides a surprisingly accurate view of trends.

Just looking at the raw month-to-month numbers in the graph below feels a little like a ride on a rollercoaster. The up and down vagaries of watching only real-time data can be disconcerting, especially with sharp downward months seen in the middle of this chart.

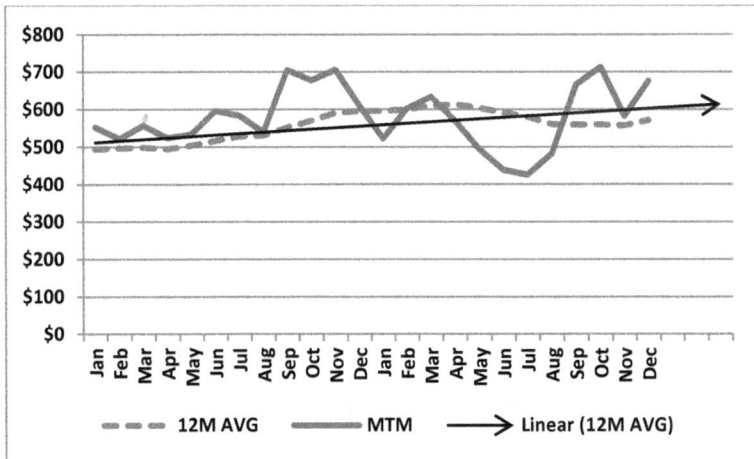

Two-Year Chart of Monthly Billing ($K)
Using 12-Month Trailing Average Model

This view of actual data is very typical of the radical changes in key indicators, including sales, billings, and opportunity dollars, and how wildly they can vary on a month-to-month basis.

However, when charted using the 12-month trailing average, the picture becomes more stable, and more predictable. Compared against budgets or goals (straight-line averages over the same period), it becomes instantly clear about which way the trend is moving. Adding a future-facing three-, six-, or nine-month linear trend line provides further clarity. In this case, both the 12-month trailing average and a six-month look-ahead trend line reinforce a positive up-tick in revenue.

Taking a data-driven look-back overlaid with a forward projection provides a valuable perspective that can show positive results early and negative change in time to make adjustments to your business strategy.

This approach has the added value, when plotted year-over-year, of showing that the overall picture, while dismal right now, is not the precipitous drop it may feel like today.

Rate of change is another good metric to chart. The month-over-month percentage change can quickly identify improvement or need for improvement, even when the raw numbers are still not where you think they should be.

However you chart your results, positive or negative results are good indicators of improving or declining brand equity.

RETURN ON INVESTMENT

Return on investment (ROI) is an interesting and important concept. In professional service firms, the cost benefit of business development is often difficult to segregate, calculate, and measure. This is not because it's a difficult concept, but because there are so many factors.

ROI is precisely measured by comparing the direct overhead costs of a single business developer (salary, benefits, bonus, expenses, etc.) against the firm's profit associated with the work that individual was responsible for or associated with. This is the typical accounting/finance perspective.

However, more often than not, there is a team of professionals responsible for the client interaction necessary to win and perform any project assignment. The contribution of any one individual to the successful contracting of a new piece of business varies widely—from introduction, to strategic overview, tactical solution, proposal, presentation, final contract negotiation, and finally, to actually performing the service— which, in turn, determines the profit.

And therein lays the challenge. How much weight do you put on the initial relationship development, when both winning and performing—and the resulting profit—are dependent on a team of professionals with varying degrees of ability? Is it fair to measure the business developer's performance on so many factors out of that individual's control? Probably not, but it remains an important metric.

Other ROI measures that may be considered in analyzing business development and brand performance include:

1. **Visibility** within your market focus or geography is measured by the actual or percent increase in number of contacts and potential clients. This can be a general measure or a market-specific measure when the firm wants to diversify or expand in a particular sector.

2. **Opportunity pipeline** is measured by the actual or percent increase in potential net fees for qualified projects (gross fees less consultants and non-billable expenses and splits with other offices or departments within the organization). The ideal depth of the opportunity pipeline is typically a calculation of the firm's success or hit ratio (see #5 below)

as the denominator to the firm's sales budget target (for example, if you win 33 percent of the work you go after, you need a visible pipeline that is three times your sales goal). This is preferable to measuring the number of opportunities, because the quantity is irrelevant if the total potential fee is not reached.

3. **Submittal-to-Shortlist** results are measured by the actual or percentage increase of success in converting statement of qualification or proposal responses to shortlist interviews. The business developer is usually not a contributor to the actual preparation of the response, but they should be a key strategist in determining the content and how to address the client's most important issues and a reviewer of the submittal for content and consistency of message. Think like the client (it is not "all about us"), because if you don't make the cut, you can't get to the win.

4. **Shortlist-to-Win** results are measured by the number of engagements or dollar value of engagements divided by the number of interviews. Again, the business developer is not usually a part of the interview team, but should contribute client-specific knowledge to the preparation and rehearsal process.

5. **Hit rate** is measured by the dollar value of wins divided by the factored (percent chance of win) dollar value opportunities in a given period (month, quarter, or year). Again, the business developer contributes, but is not totally responsible for this effort. This is where the work that is performed starts, with profits as the result. You can't design, build, or bill it, if you don't win it first.

For smaller, niche firms, quantity ratios make the most sense if project fees are predictably consistent. For larger firms where project fees vary greatly, dollar-based ratios are more relevant.

In a challenging marketplace, all of these ROI factors are critical. Showing improvement in any one of these factors is a positive metric of a business developer's value. Improvement in all is a metric of the firm's overall marketing, business development, and public relations efforts. But, improvement in the profit/cost ratio is still the measure that pays the rent, salaries, benefits, and bonuses. Bottom line: they all matter.

THE ODDS OF WINNING

Moving relationships to opportunities and opportunities to projects are the fundamental goals of the brand as executed by the marketer and business developer. The steps along the way confirm the depth and breadth of the relationship (who), back-story (why), and details of the opportunity (what, when, and how much) and support the calculation of brand equity.

Those same steps can provide the metrics for judging the progress of moving a potential opportunity from unqualified to qualified to proposal to presentation to contract—all key measures of brand value and business development effectiveness.

When asked the likelihood of winning a piece of work, business developers often say, *"50/50"*—we will or we won't. Many will say, *"There are four contenders, so we have a 25 percent chance."* The percentage varies with the depth of competition. The less confident will say, *"We don't know enough yet"*—usually right up until the project is awarded to someone else.

Those answers are all rarely true. While there are many potential factors that go into your decision to pursue a project or client, there are a few simple qualities that can quickly and easily define your likelihood of winning.

Using the criteria listed below, a percentage chance of winning a pursuit can be calculated based on whom, why, what, when, and how much you know.

- **Possible** (10 to 30 percent chance): You know about the opportunity, but not enough detail to speak to scope, schedule, or budget. Cumulative values are assigned as follows:
  - You have worked for the client before (10 percent)
  - You have successfully completed a similar assignment before (20 percent)

- You have successfully completed a similar assignment for this client before (30 percent).

If you cannot answer *yes* to any of these three initial criteria questions, you have no business pursuing the project and are probably wasting your time and money. Spend it more wisely learning to do your work better, expanding your services with your existing client base, and building your relationships with this client to position for a pursuit that you have a better calculated chance of winning in the future.

That is not to say you should not submit to a potential client that you have not worked for in the past. However, be aware your chances are slim (or more likely none), unless you have invested the time to get to know that client and all the internal decision makers and influencers before you make that first submittal.

- **Potential** (31 to 50 percent chance): You can say yes to the three criteria above and you know the scope, schedule, and budget the client has established for the project:
  - A higher value is given if your experts have demonstrated your expertise to the client within three to six months before the request for proposal (40 percent).
  - If your relationship is deep and current, or you have been recommended to the client by a referral from your past work for another (similar) client, move up the ladder (50 percent).

A long history and a strong portfolio may get you to the shortlist, but your odds of winning are significantly less than those competitors the client actually knows. Again, if the answer is no, or less than perfect, consider investing additional time in research and relationship building before submitting.

- **Probable** (51 to 90 percent): Now comes the hard part. Getting to the contract requires a win strategy that speaks authentically to the client's goals. It is not enough just to know the scope, schedule, and budget.

    - You've done a project *"just like this"* successfully for another client (70 percent)

    - You've done this successfully for multiple clients (80 percent)

    - You've done this for this client and multiple other clients (90 percent)

You also need to know the back-story—why does the client need this project completed? What difference will it make to their enterprise? How will that difference be measured?

Most importantly, how can you articulate an understanding of these key issues and demonstrate how you have successfully addressed them in the past? What will differentiate your specific and relevant knowledge, experience, and approach from the competition?

Finally, do you have a strong relationship with all of the stakeholders on the client's side (internal and influential)? If the answer is *"yes,"* move up to 95 percent; if the answer is *"limited"* or *"no,"* subtract 10 percent.

How do you get to 100 percent probability? What about that final 5 percent? Unfortunately, there are always intangibles that influence outcomes. They may include the client's ability to fund or approve the project. There may be changes in the client's organization or in the larger economy impacting the client's business and ability to move forward with the project.

There may be a competitor you don't know (or know about) prepared to offer a better solution, price, or schedule. As marketing leaders, it is your job to know these intangibles and prepare for them.

To respond to the unknown, scenario planning should be a key part of any win strategy, with appropriate counter-measures identified and prepared.

Beyond those strategies, there remains the skill to closing the deal. Frankly, it is less a skill than an outcome based entirely on the breadth and depth of your relationship with the client's key stakeholders. You can ask and receive a predictive *"yes"* when you know them well and they know you.

And, you can ask and receive a qualified *"maybe"* when you don't. You increase the chances of the possible becoming potential and the potential becoming probable exponentially when you put your efforts into strengthening your business-to-business relationships.

ON RESULTS

However you define your key metrics, recognize that predictive analytics is an art as much as a science, but definitely one that should be at the heart of demonstrating the results of your brand-building and brand-equity tracking strategies.

Demonstrating foresight is critical to delivering results. Measuring and reporting trends and results will give you credibility with management more than any other creative marketing or branding effort.

The Architecture of Image

PSI: *One Company, One Call*

PSI (Professional Service Industries, Inc.) is a provider of geotechnical, construction material testing, environmental, and related engineering services for clients buying, selling, managing, and developing real estate. The firm is categorized as a generalist— not tied to a specific vertical market.

Founded in 1881, PSI is one of the nation's largest engineering firms—with 2,500 people working in 100 offices spanning 34 states—providing engineering, scientific, technical, and management solutions to public and private sector clients involved with site selection, design, construction, and property management. PSI also provides a variety of specialty engineering and testing services to business and industry.

PSI's brand identity is based on a set of core values they define as SQES (Safety, Quality, Ethics, and Sales), Delight, and Profitability. They believe that if they follow the mission of SQES, and, as a result, delight their clients, the profitability will naturally follow. Their taglines—*"Information to Build On"* and *"One Company, One*

Call"—reflect a brand promise of their ability to unify solutions through a variety of different services.

Tom Boogher, CPSM, executive vice president and CMO, commented on the importance of brand, *"I think we have an excellent reputation, but are often misunderstood for the breadth and depth of the services we provide. Our challenge is to increase our client's awareness of all we can do for them, in contrast to how we might be perceived for a particular service that they may have contracted us for."*

PSI surveys 1,000 to 1,500 clients monthly as part of their SQES client satisfaction program. It is driven at the local level by operations managers who are required to survey a minimum of 10 clients every month. This creates a scorecard that is tied to their incentive program. He noted that it is a fairly short form survey, done in person on the phone. They don't use electronic surveys because they feel it is more important to have the conversation with the client directly.

Like many firms as large as PSI, having every employee able to state the brand promise of benefits and values is a challenge, even at the leadership level. He noted that as a differentiator or "so what" statement, his goal is to improve that ability across the firm.

Three words define PSI's brand image: dependable, responsive, and competitive. These reflect their goals for the firm.

Like many firms in the building industry, PSI focuses on hiring bright people with the right degrees and licenses and the right experience. However, they acknowledge that on an expertise level in a client's mind, they are similar to other firms and often somewhat interchangeable. As a differentiator, PSI has developed some proprietary systems that drive how they deliver information.

Boogher believes differentiators are earned by your service, and how you interact and touch your clients. It is their experience that differentiates you from the competition, which is more important than technical expertise.

PSI has acquired more than 90 firms in their 30 years, though that has become less important than organic growth in the last 5 years. They have a fast integration process, averaging 3 to 9 months from old name to PSI. They do not waste a lot of time.

PSI leadership sees an opportunity to break down the silos within the company and get their clients to understand how PSI can provide other services and support their needs in different geographies. This is an excellent example of a brand-oriented goal.

.

AFTERWORD | **You Are *The New Black!***

A great brand is a story that's never completely told.
SCOTT BEDBURY

A BRAND PROMISE IS JUST THAT, *a promise*. Every member of your firm should be able to answer two questions, *"What is our brand promise? What will I do today to keep that promise?"*

Management guru Tom Peters' position is that the brand is shorthand for the promise of reliable action and trust.[13] Peters postulates that in an era of downsizing, off-shoring, and realignment—note that those same factors really haven't changed much in recent years—the only hope for the individual or the professional service is to take a lesson from other brand leaders and create the brand *YOU* for your firm and for yourself as a marketing leader.

So, while you may be a part of a larger organization and you may be invested in the practices outlined here for building your firm's brand, you can easily build your personal brand while still supporting the larger goals of your employer.

---

[13] Peters, Tom, *The Brand Called YOU, Fast Company*, August 1997.

The Architecture of Image

Like the exterior skin of a building, your brand is the culmination of all the steps described here. Your brand is who you are as perceived by the world. It is the client's definition of your *image.* And, it *begins* with your *culture.*

Lippincott's Wilke says, *"It starts with making sure you really have clarity about your own brand. You have to know who you are, what you stand for, and how you are different. We can use fancy branding terms like positioning or value proposition, but at the end of the day you need to know what the marketplace thinks of you."*

Your brand *builds* on how you *collaborate* with your clients, with your professional cohorts, and with your vendors and suppliers.

Tracy Black, says, *"While at a simplistic level, brand may be seen as visible manifestations, such as your logo, your letterhead, or your website—graphics play only a supporting role for your brand."*

More importantly, your brand is your thought leadership, your innovation, and your willingness and success at leading the collaborative process of delivering your professional service.

How you *communicate* and measure your results define what your brand *becomes*. Your brand is communicated through your public relations, publications, and public speaking. It reflects your understanding of your clients' business models, the changes in their processes, and how your service can help them succeed.

Wilke adds, *"Ten years ago, branding professional services was seen as a nice thing to do. Seven years ago, it became a first-mover advantage. Now, if you haven't done it, you're lagging behind and you're playing catch up."*

Addressing the issues of culture will help keep your brand aligned with your firm's needs and goals, and give you the ability to accurately measure results.

Webster's Musil concurs, *"For metrics, we have our clients look for an uptick in new clients or quality of clients, or size of clients that result from the branding effort. However, this is often anecdotal and while tied to increased business, it more revolves around that word 'buzz.'"*

The Architecture of Image

But your brand is really much more. Your brand demonstrates your passion for your area of practice and leadership in your profession. When you go out into the market, existing or new, your brand is the buzz about you.

Black notes, *"The brand effort doesn't take loyalty for granted. It knows it as a gift. To build and maintain your brand will take consistent, timely, regular, and continuing effort of refinement and development. Building an effective brand is an ongoing, evolutionary process."*

Musil adds, *"For the professional service, your brand is based on what you do and it is not something that is easily quantifiable. It is not something the client can touch and is often less than obvious. It requires a more abstract approach to selling. For those individuals representing a company in business development, they must be the personification of the company's brand."*

Market dynamics, political and demographic changes, and societal needs will continue to challenge your practice. Competitors will develop new services, communicate value better, and push you to grow. Clients will, too. Hopefully, you will act first. Status quo is for the follower, not the leader. And as all things change, so will your brand.

And, so—consistent with my postulate on the power of three with which I began the book—I conclude with three ideas to remember:

1. **Know your market; know your culture.** Expertise, experience, and proven excellence define your niche—be happy for that. The challenge when opportunities are slim is chasing after anything that smells like work. Unfortunately, many succumb to fear and waste good energy on bad behavior. Revisit your culture's vision and values and spend time researching clients and their clients who align with your strengths. Knowledge trumps unfocused activity every time.

2. **Respect your network; collaborate to win.** Everyone in professional services, regardless of specialty, is in the same boat: fewer projects, more competition, and downward fee pressure. Invest time connecting and reconnecting with those you know, whether they can bring you business or lead you to business. Learn what they see, share what you know, seek commonalities, and consider jointly beneficial strategies.

3. **Tell your story; communicate value.** Even with fewer projects, there are still projects to talk about. Leverage the media ("All PR is good PR!") and share challenges, benefits and proofs with your clients, potential clients, and their clients and your communities. When times are slow, building your media network is as critical as building your pipeline.

The Architecture of Image

According to SMPS' Worth, *"Your culture is your brand. The number one concern expressed by clients today is that you will do what you say you are going do. That does not mean only faster or cheaper—simply do what you say. What the clients want most is to believe your brand promise."*

ON THE ARCHITECTURE OF IMAGE

Your goal and brand promise should be to recognize your culture's unique traits, find how you can collaborate to build brand equity, and learn how you can communicate the value of your brand to your clients. You will build your brand and grow your practice.

Begin with a vision aligned with your *culture*, *build* a strong brand by *collaborating* in the delivery of your promise, and *become* the brand you envision by *communicating* your value every day throughout your organization.

The result will be the foundation for a unique brand and an enduring practice that provides you, your staff, your firm, and your clients with a memorable—and *remarkable*—experience!

RECOMMENDED READING

Here are other books that I think you will find useful in building and developing the brand of your firm:

- Beckwith, Harry, and Christine Beckwith, *You, Inc.: The Art of Selling Yourself*, New York, NY: Hachette Book Group, 2006.
- Beckwith, Harry, *The Invisible Touch: The Four Keys to Modern Marketing*, New York, NY: Warner Books, 2000.
- Beckwith, Harry, *Selling the Invisible: A Field Guide to Modern Marketing*, New York, NY: Warner Books, 1997.
- Bedbury, Scott, *A New Brand World: 8 Principals for Achieving Brand Leadership in the 21st Century*, New York, NY: Viking, 2002.
- Bell, Greg, **Water the Bamboo: Unleashing the Potential of Teams and Individuals,** Portland, OR: Three Star Publishing, 2009.
- Brogan, Chris, *Trust Agents: Using the Web to Build Influence, Improve Reputation, and Earn Trust*, Hoboken, NJ: John Wiley & Sons, 2009.
- D'Alessandro, David and Michele Owens, *Brand Warfare: 10 Rules for Building the Killer Brand,* New York, NY: McGraw-Hill, 2001.
- Dawson, Ross, *Developing Knowledge-Based Client Relationships: The Future of Professional Services*, Boston, MA: Butterworth-Heinemann, 2000.
- Farris, Paul; Neil Bendle; Phillip Pfeifer; David Reibstein, *Marketing Metrics: The Definitive Guide to Measuring Marketing Performance*, Upper Saddle River, New Jersey: Pearson Education, Inc., 2010.

- Fugere, Brian, C. Hardaway and J. Warshawsky, *Why Business People Speak Like Idiots: A Bullfighter's Guide*, New York, NY: Free Press, 2005.

- Gobé, Marc, *Emotional Branding: The New Paradigm for Connecting Brands to People*, New York, NY: Allworth Press, 2001.

- Graham, Stedman, *Build Your Own Brand: A Powerful Strategy to Maximize Your Potential and Enhance Your Value for Ultimate Achievement*, New York, NY: The Free Press, 2001.

- Haig, Matt, *Brand Royalty: How the World's Top 100 Brands Thrive & Survive*, London: Kogan Page, 2004.

- Hiebler, Robert, Thomas Kelly and Charles Ketteman, *Best Practices: Building Your Business with Customer-Focused Solutions*, New York, NY: Simon & Shuster, 1998.

- Kaputa, Catherine, *You Are the Brand!: How Smart People Brand Themselves for Business Success*, Boston, MA: Nicholas Brealy Publishing, 2010.

- Kubal, Michael, Kevin Miller & Ronald Worth, *Building Profits in The Construction Industry*, New York, NY: McGraw-Hill Book Company, 1999.

- Lindstrom, Martin and Philip Kotler, *Brand Sense: Build Powerful Brands through Touch, Taste, Smell, Sight and Sound*, New York, NY: The Free Press, 2005.

- Miles, Josh, *Bold Brand: The New Rules for Differentiating, Branding, and Marketing Your Professional Service Firm*, Cleveland, OH: Content Marketing Institute, 2012.

- Neumeier, Marty, *The Brand Gap: How to Bridge the Distance between Business Strategy and Design*, Berkeley, CA: New Riders Publishing, 2003.

- Peters, Tom, *The Brand You 50*, New York, NY: Alfred A. Knopf, Inc., 1999.

- Peters, Tom, *The Professional Service Firm 50*, New York, NY: Alfred A. Knopf, Inc., 1999.
- Post, Karen, **Brain Tattoos: Creating Unique Brands That Stick in Your Customer's Minds**, New York, NY: AMACOM, 2005.
- Potter, Robert, *Winning in the Invisible Market: A Guide to Selling Professional Services in Turbulent Times*, San Francisco, CA: RA Potter Advisors, 2003.
- Reis, Al and Laura Reis, *The 22 Immutable Laws of Branding: How to Build a Product or Service into a World Class Brand,* New York, NY: Harper Press, 2002.
- Reis, All and Jack Trout, *Positioning: The Battle for Your Mind*, New York, NY: McGraw-Hill, 2001.
- Richards, Brenda and Kathleen Soldati, *Business Comes to the Expert: A Proactive Marketing Plan for Professional Practice Firms,* Norcross, GA: Ostberg Library of Design Management, 2008.
- SMPS, *The Marketing Handbook for Design & Construction Professionals,* Alexandria: BNi, 3rd Edition, 2009.
- Trout, Jack and Steve Rivkin, *Differentiate or Die: Survival in Our Era of Killer Competition*, New York, NY: John Wiley & Sons, 2000.
- Waters, Robyn, *The Trendmaster's Guide: Get a Jump on What Your Customer Wants Next*, New York, NY: Portfolio, 2005.
- Webster, Bryce, *The Power of Consultative Selling*, Paramus, NJ: Prentice Hall, 1987.
- Weiss, Alan, *How to Establish a Unique Brand in the Consulting Profession*, Danvers, MA: Jossey-Bass/Pfeiffer, 2002.
- Wheeler, Alina, *Designing Brand Identity: A Complete Guide to Creating, Building, and Maintaining Strong Brands*, Hoboken, NJ: John Wiley & Sons, 2006.
- Winsor, John, *Beyond the Brand: Why Engaging the Right Customers is Essential to Winning in Business*, Chicago, IL: Dearborn Publishing, 2004.

INDEX TO CONTRIBUTORS

Banning-Wright, Ann   xvii, 31, 38, 39, 151, 212

Barrick, Tim   xvii, 141-144, 150, 212

Black, Tracy   xvi, 36, 39, 40, 42, 55-59, 132-134, 164, 174-179, 197, 198, 200, 211

Boogher, Tom   xvii, 35, 77, 110, 119, 146, 174, 192, 212

Luers, Julie   xvii, 5, 6, 76, 80, 82, 114, 115, 120, 212

Maffry, Maria   xvii, 8, 22, 26, 64, 79, 212

Musil, Dick   xix, 3, 16, 25, 43, 118, 152, 199, 200, 212

Powell-Caldwell, Teresa   xvii, 5, 8, 167-170, 212

Reilly, Mike   xix, 7, 15, 98, 107, 147, 148, 160, 212

Savage, Mike   xvii, 10, 76, 90, 91, 212

Thompson, Carla   xvii, 4, 20, 45-49, 78, 87, 132, 212

Watson, Chris   xvii, 82, 101-104, 156, 212

Wilke, Richard   xix, 2, 4, 11, 53, 108-110, 198, 199, 212

Worth, Ron   i-iv, xviii, 2, 9, 11, 55, 76, 83, 109, 148, 202, 212

The Architecture of Image

BRAND WEB LINKS

Links to companies and organizations referenced herein or that were cited during the book's development for their authenticity, consistency, and value reflected in their brand promise.

AECOM | aecom.com

Archimania | archimania.com

Architect One | architectonepa.com

Arup | arup.com

Barbara Barry Inc. | barbarabarry.com

Black Cape Marketing | blackcapemarketing.com

BNIM | bnim.com

Bright Operations | brightoperations.com

BSA Lifestructures | bsalifestructures.com

Burns & McDonnell | burnsmcd.com

Buro Happold | burohappold.com

DPR | dprinc.com

Gafcon | gafcon.com

Gensler | gensler.com

Geotechnologies | geoteq.com

Gilbane Building Company | gilbaneco.com

Harley Ellis Devereaux | hedev.com

HDR | hdrinc.com

HGA | hga.com

Hnedak Bobo Group | hbginc.com

HNTB | hntb.com

Kleinfelder | kleinfelder.com

LEO A DALY | leoadaly.com

Lippincott | lippincott.com

Morley Builders |
morleybuilders.com

Mortensen Construction |
mortensen.com

MulvannyG2 |
mulvannyg2.com

Perkins+Will |
perkinswill.com

PlanNet Consulting |
plannet.net

Populous | populous.com

PSI | psiusa.com

RATIO Architects |
ratioarchitects.com

Reilly Communications |
reillycommunications.com

Skanska | skanska.com

SLAM Collaborative |
slamcoll.com

Society for Marketing
Professional Services |
smps.org

Structural Focus |
structuralfocus.com

Syska Hennessy Group |
syska.com

The Sextant Group |
thesextantgroup.com

Thornton Tomasetti |
thorntontomasetti.com

Turner |
turnerconstruction.com

Webster |
websterdesign.com

Walter P Moore |
walterpmoore.com

Water the Bamboo Center
for Leadership |
waterthebamboo.com

WET | wetdesign.com

ACKNOWLEDGEMENTS

When words are both kind and true,
they can change the world.
BUDDHA

THIS BOOK STARTED WITH INSPIRATION, then research, time—in this case, lots of it—input from experts, and finally the author's creative output, followed quickly and most importantly by a keen editorial eye, and then the validation from respected colleagues that the topic is sound. I was lucky to have all of those steps supported with grace and generosity from those whose input helped make this book a reality.

The inspiration came unexpectedly from a meeting with Gabriele Lucci, founder of the International Academy of Image Arts & Sciences in L'Aquila, Italy. He had asked me to give a talk on the subject of the architecture of image, related to the application of visual media in building design. It struck me that the same topic could equally describe the brand development process of a professional service. Not only did this meeting start the book, but my subsequent visit to the Institute's home city gave birth to the name for my publishing company, Aquilan Press.

The Architecture of Image

With my thinking focused on the service firm's brand challenge, I read extensively on the topic of brand and drafted the initial manuscript. I then reached out to several of my friends and cohorts for their insight and wisdom. The results you see here.

First, I must sincerely thank my friend Tracy Black, president of Black Cape Marketing. As one of the editors of my first book, *The Architecture of Value: Building Your Professional Practice*, Tracy established herself as more than capable in helping with the organization, content, structure, and the blocking and tackling of grammar and punctuation.

For *The Architecture of Image*, Tracy provided invaluable insight and contributions on the connection between service provider, client, and community, and the methods of making those brand connections. As always, she brought an extraordinary editorial gift that has made this a better read than I ever imagined.

I also thank my "expert" contributors: Mike Reilly and Dick Musil for their sage input on this diverse topic. Equally, I thank Ann Banning-Wright, Tim Barrick, Tom Boogher, Julie Luers, Maria Maffry, Teresa Powell-Caldwell, Mike Savage, Carla Thompson, and Chris Watson for their willingness to share the stories of the branding initiatives at their companies.

I am also grateful for the insight of Richard Wilke, whose big picture views from the lofty brand tower at Lippincott—drawn from our *Marketer* cover story interview—provide an invaluable perspective from one of the global pinnacles of marketing thought leadership.

And, I am ever indebted to Ron Worth, CEO of the Society for Marketing Professional Services, for both his Foreword to the book and his input to its content. Ron is an icon in the professional service marketing universe and I am as honored by his friendship as I am for his succinct praise for my ideas and his approach to the ideas of building the brand of the professional service firm.

Special thanks go to my good friend, Scott Lindsay, for providing a more-than-comfortable alternative to the proverbial "poor artist's garret" by letting me use his beautiful little Gate House as the site for my initial research and writing. That first week alone provided much needed focus and his encouragement helped set the tone and spirit of the content.

ABOUT THE AUTHOR

*In every man's writings, the character
of the writer must lie recorded.*
THOMAS CARLYLE

CRAIG PARK, FSMPS, ASSOC. AIA has been
active in the building industry for more
than 30 years, holding strategic marketing
leadership roles for firms in design and
engineering consulting, contracting, and
manufacturing.

He received a bachelor of science in architecture from California
State Polytechnic University, San Luis Obispo, and completed
post-graduate continuing education programs at New York
University and the Advanced Management Institute in San
Francisco.

Park is a Fellow, past national president, Weld Coxe Marketing
Achievement Award recipient, and Distinguished Life Member of
the Society for Marketing Professional Services. He is also active
in the American Institute of Architects and InfoComm
International.

Additional information on strategic marketing intelligence is
available on his websites: craigpark.com and thevirtualcmo.com.
For more information on publishing professional service thought
leadership, visit aquilanpress.com.

www.ingramcontent.com/pod-product-compliance
Lightning Source LLC
Chambersburg PA
CBHW072101020426

42334CB00017B/1593